CW00972367

This edition published in 2018 by Hardie Grant Books,
an imprint of Hardie Grant Publishing

First published in 2018 by Éditions Marabout (Hachette Livre)

Hardie Grant Books (Melbourne)
Building 1, 658 Church Street
Richmond, Victoria 3121

Hardie Grant Books (London)
5th & 6th Floors
52–54 Southwark Street
London SE1 1UN

hardiegrantbooks.com

All rights reserved. No part of this publication may be reproduced, stored
in a retrieval system or transmitted in any form by any means, electronic,
mechanical, photocopying, recording or otherwise, without the prior written
permission of the publishers and copyright holders.

The moral rights of the author have been asserted.

Copyright text © Éditions Marabout (Hachette Livre), 2018
Copyright design © Éditions Marabout (Hachette Livre), 2018

A catalogue record for this book is available from the National Library of Australia.

The Book of Ikigai
ISBN 978 1 74379 494 4

10 9 8 7 6 5 4 3 2 1

Cover design: Vanessa Masci
Design: Le Gall & Chassagnard

Colour reproduction by Splitting Image Colour Studio
Printed in China by Leo Paper Product. LTD

Contents

kigai is a Japanese word. It's made up of four characters that mean 'life', 'what's worth doing', 'priority and initiative' and 'beauty and elegance'. In short, it means having a good reason to get up in the morning. Bringing sense to your life and making it joyful. It's a beautiful idea: after all, isn't it the meaning of life that motivates us to live? And doesn't living fully mean experiencing joy in our everyday life?

The concept comes from Okinawa, a Japanese island known for its surprising number of centenarians. Recent studies show that apart from the well-known Okinawan diet, the islanders have another secret: each is encouraged to find and achieve their *ikigai*.

Ikigai simultaneously implies the idea of self-actualisation and the notion of contributing to society. It's so culturally important in Japan that many people continue to work after retirement. For example, by tending the rice paddies, older people draw great pleasure from the outdoors, pass on respect for nature to younger generations and nourish their family, while continuing to feel vibrant and useful.

Younger Japanese, no longer wanting to work themselves into the ground like their ancestors, are prioritising their *ikigai* above everything else. Many thirty-somethings have renounced social success, preferring to pursue their ideals, and resigned to earning less. These young people are quite poorly regarded by older generations, who find them lazy and treat them like *karyû* – shirkers. Despite this bad reputation, the *karyû* are much happier than those who criticise them.

Ikigai is a compass that guides each person through a life they consider to be good and worthwhile; to know a life that brings them individual satisfaction while opening them up to a cause greater than themselves.

Why find your *ikigai*? In these unsettled times when so many of us continually change jobs, retraining and adapting, it's vital to bring some sense to it all; to know why we're here and what we want to give to the world. It's exactly what we need.

My grandmother, who was an expert in Taoist medicine and Kabbalah, said to me one day: 'I've done everything I came for.' Not long afterwards, she passed away. Her *ikigai* was to discover an alternative to Western medicine and she accomplished her mission. Once she believed that she had given everything she could, she no longer had any reason to live. Literally. I always had great admiration for this driven woman, who was willing to climb mountains to reach her goal. At the time, not yet having discovered my own goal, I thought I could never be like her. I've since found my goal – it's to discover new ways of being happy and make them accessible to everyone. Now I'm outdoing myself, just as she did.

Fulfilling our potential is the best thing we can offer to society. Imagine a world where everyone loves their job and goes there singing. Do you think that's crazy? What I find crazy is that this sounds like a utopia.

How do you find your *ikigai*? It demands a long investigation into yourself; it's more an intuitive search than an intellectual one. It takes time. Looking at the world through new eyes; giving yourself up to activities that seem 'useless'; letting yourself live, no longer fearing that you're wasting time; accepting boredom, slowness, calm. It's through emptying yourself, in every way, that you'll find your *ikigai*.

I think of this book as an interlude. Time you can give yourself to reflect, but above all to feel – to experiment in small doses, just enough that it can become part of your everyday life without disrupting it too much. It's broken up into twelve weeks, covering varied themes that will gradually allow you to get to know yourself better. Through participating in a number of fun – and sometimes surprising – games, you'll start to piece together the puzzle that is the mystery of your *ikigai*.

Get yourself a pretty notebook to accompany you through this journey. Take plenty of time to complete each exercise, even – perhaps most importantly – those that don't really tempt you at first glance. They have much to teach you, so stay open. Conduct this enquiry as if it's about someone else, a stranger you must get to know. Let yourself be surprised and open yourself up, little by little, to the path that will make your life light, joyful and enriching.

I'M RECONNECTING WITH MYSELF

This week, it's essential, if you're to make progress in your quest towards your *ikigai*, to reconnect with yourself.

How can we make sense of life if we can't manage to recognise our own daily needs? You are not looking for the Holy Grail: the answer is within you, so rediscovering your interior dialogue is an important step.

The Japanese inspiration this week will be finding pleasure in the moment and connecting with nature.

This week, we'll also look at pathways you need to renew within yourself, particularly within your body. **Because the good news is that even if you no longer know what you need, your body does.**

Let's rediscover quality of being.

Let's think a little

This is the story of a girl who had no idea what she wanted. She was without joy, without passion, without motivation. She wandered through life without really knowing what purpose that served, let alone what purpose she served. She adapted herself to others to try and be accepted. And so she never asked herself what she really wanted or needed. She contented herself with following along, enduring her dreary daily life – although it seemed shiny enough – while hoping that, one day, things would miraculously change. Just as some women wait for their Prince Charming, she waited for a revelation, a voice that would say, 'Here's what you were made for', 'Here's the meaning of your life.' She had an excellent education and was gifted in every subject. The careers counsellor told her: 'Study the sciences. You're talented.' She was unconvinced of this, but neither did she feel particularly literary, so she took the middle road, lazily, and chose economics. What to study after school? She never knew how to answer that question, leaning at the last minute towards the arts, without any great conviction.

That girl was me. And the first stage of my radical shift away from that person into who I am today – which took three years – was to learn that I have a body. And what's more, that it has things to tell me.

Robot mode

Are you a robot? The majority of us will answer 'no' to this question, of course. Let's play a little game. Take a piece of paper and a pencil. You have fifteen seconds to draw a flower.

Quick, quick!
Come on, hurry!
Done?
What does your flower look like?
Is it a daisy?
This daisy?

If so, you have, like 95 per cent of the people I've given this exercise to, opted for the commonly accepted image of a flower. It's a flower that's understood by everyone.
Did you enjoy drawing it?
Not really, eh?

And if you could now draw your preferred flower?
Take your time, without pressure. We're not expecting something we could sell at an art gallery, just a flower that you love, a flower drawn in your own way. Even if it's clumsy, we don't care. It's just for pleasure.

How long did that take you?
Fifteen seconds? Twenty seconds? Not much longer, I imagine.
I hope, above all, that it did you good.
If it did, then why didn't you draw that flower the first time I asked?
Because you were in what I call **'robot mode'**.

What does that mean?

It means that when you find yourself under pressure, you don't take the time to ask yourself what pleases you. You do what's expected. You could have drawn a tulip or a lotus flower: it's no more complicated, and even the worst of artists could manage it in fifteen seconds.

Then why did you draw a daisy?

Because you didn't take the time to ask yourself: 'Hang on, what's my favourite flower?' or even 'What flower would I like to draw?' Because you were in a hurry. We were expecting a drawing from you in a short time and you did the simplest one you could, setting pleasure, joy and inclination aside. That's also probably what you do in your life, every day, without even noticing.

Gratuitous pleasure

The best way to resume contact with your desires is to get there via gratuitous pleasure. When was the last time you did something that was truly unproductive? What about something that was completely useless?

Do you allow yourself emptiness?

In a world moving at two hundred kilometres an hour, knowing how to stop just for pleasure is a real talent. It means daring to go against the flow. Imagine a Formula 1 driver stopping his car on the side of the road to look at a butterfly. He would be booed, criticised, threatened. He would put himself in danger and set off a chain of reactions and terrible mockery.

The good news is that you're not a race car driver. And nor is there a track. Yes, the world moves quickly. Yes, we need to move with it. But there's nothing really preventing us from saying 'stop'. I know what you'll say. 'But I don't have enough time. I have to earn a living. I'm in danger of losing my job.' And as soon as you start going down that road, I'll be the one saying 'stop'. Stopping is not about going off to meditate in an Indian ashram without an internet connection. It's about doing small pleasurable things every day that serve no purpose. It's so difficult for us to be unproductive that I bet you're going to think of lots of pleasures that are still too useful.

Making a cake won't work, because you'll eat it, and it will bring pleasure to those around you. Generally speaking, cooking doesn't work because it serves to nourish us. Sport? No, that doesn't work either. That gets you in shape, and so it's very useful. You see, you've really lost the habit. It's something children do naturally … all the time. But you don't even know what it is anymore.

Do you need inspiration?
Here are some funny little unproductive things I do, which you could use as a starting point, and then very quickly you'll find your own:
● Scribble on a piece of paper, then screw it into a ball and throw it in the bin as if it's basketball.
● Draw on the rim of the bathtub using just water, or some shower gel.
● Lie down and watch the clouds, looking for funny shapes.
● Jump into puddles.
● Put on some music and sing along, using a hairbrush as a microphone.

How can we forget to listen to ourselves?

It seems crazy that we could forget to listen to ourselves. It's a very simple idea: listening, being attentive to our own needs and knowing our own desires. Yet the majority of us are incapable of doing it. Why? Apart from time pressures, which we explored with the example of the flower, there are other factors that prevent us from this kind of self-reflection.

● **Education:** Our parents, who only wanted the best for us, made lots of decisions for us, without consulting us or really listening to us. For example: 'Put on your sweater!' 'No, I'm hot.' 'Put on your sweater, it's cold.' Or 'It's bedtime.' 'I'm not tired.' 'Go to bed, you're tired.' As a result, we started turning to other people to know our needs: these other people took possession of the truth – and because our feelings didn't fit in with this truth, we stopped listening to them.

● **Social pressure:** Watching ourselves, listening to ourselves and taking care of ourselves is rather poorly regarded. It creates an image of egotism and self-centredness.

● **Ignorance:** No one told us – in primary school, in high school, wherever it was – that it's essential to know your own needs. As a result, we don't take the time and we don't offer ourselves this option, since we don't know it's necessary or, indeed, that it's even possible. Even if we did hear people talk about the necessity of listening to ourselves, we didn't know how to go about it.

Need a holiday?

Why is your life so different when you're on holiday? Why is it so much nicer? Okay, you're not working. If we start from the principle that your work is a constraint – which isn't always true – on holiday you're set free.

But beyond that?

Holidays are time away from the habitual commotion of your daily existence. They mean no time pressure – except for those who are so addicted to time pressure that they manage to stress themselves out because their holidays pass too quickly or they are already almost over. They mean no stress. And above all, no obligations. Holidays require you to make a choice: lounge around, playing the tourist in your own town; leave for a beach at the other end of the world; or discover a culture that interests you ...

Beforehand and in the moment, you're actually obliged to ask yourself the questions you avoid in your daily life. What do you need? What do you want? Not only are you listening – 'Hold on, I'd like a cocktail. Let's meet up at the bar' – but you're also allowing yourself to indulge in the things you'd otherwise treat as a whim.

Each day, you make lots of small decisions that are up to you because you no longer have any – or very few (children, travelling buddy, husband, boyfriend) – constraints. Each day, you listen to yourself: 'Would I like to go swimming?'; 'Mmm, I'm hungry. What do I feel like eating?'; 'Am I going to go out and visit a temple or sleep beside the pool?' On holidays, you feel marvellously well. What if you could bring that attitude back from your holiday rather than your umpteenth mug?

You can't bring back the sea or the mountain.
You can't bring back the sun or the waterfalls.
But your holiday attitude is completely transferable to your everyday life.

Before you panic, let's clarify what we're talking about:
● Listening to your own needs.
● Being aware of your desires.
● Following your intuition.
● Choosing what really pleases you.
● Being open to novelty and adventure.

For example?
On holiday, you decide to walk to the next village just for fun. Then, even though a friend is waiting for you to have coffee, you go into that cute little church in search of a little cool and quiet, resigned to arriving five minutes late. When you get to the cafe, you order a grenadine – yes, it's full of sugar, but after all, you've earned it!

In your daily life, you always get to work by taking the same train/bus/route. You never stop on the way, you walk quickly and you avoid all distractions so you can arrive on time.

How would an everyday holiday work?
'Hmm, this morning I'd like to walk, so I'll leave a little earlier. Hold on, I've never noticed this bakery. Oh, that smells good! Hello, one pain au chocolat, please. And how about I sit on this bench with a view of the park to eat it? These flowering trees are incredible. Uh-oh, it's already 8.55. A little sprint should get me there on time. What a pleasure this morning energy is!'

In your opinion, which of these commutes is more likely to have you arriving to work in a good mood, ready to be extra productive?

Returning to your body

How do you listen to yourself? How do you know what you really want and/or need? You just have to listen to your body.

The first time someone said to me: 'Listen to your body', I almost laughed in their face. Then, out of tactfulness, I stopped myself. No, but really: listen to a part of myself that doesn't even speak? Absurd!

Then one day, while wandering along the banks of a lake in Lausanne, I had the sudden urge to go swimming. Until that point, I was officially a coward who was afraid of cold water, and the water in this lake was less than 20°C, even in the middle of August. On paper, there was nothing about the experience for me to find pleasurable: silt disgusts me and the Loch Ness Monster haunts me. But all these negative pieces of information my brain was sending me, its cry of despair – *don't go in!* – and its last attempt at dissuasion – *but what will everyone think? Be sensible and stay where you are* – did not feel as right as this desire, which I decided to listen to.

Thank goodness, because that day I enjoyed one of the most extraordinary moments of my existence: I experienced the intense pleasure of swimming, multiplied by my pride in having overcome my fear; the feeling of merging with nature; and, above all, the jubilation of my body, that wanted freedom and cool water. It was on that day that I understood what listening to your body means. It's simply about listening to your spontaneous desires and not allowing second thoughts to sabotage them by making them impossible, inaccessible or ridiculous.

But why does my brain want to stop me from being happy? The role of reflection is to calm the body so you can avoid actions that could put you in danger and to allow you to make better choices. It's a very useful function. Except we lend so much credibility to the intellect, and so little to the body, that too often we end up choosing immobility. Reconnecting with our bodies allows us to restore balance. You are not being asked to live like a wild thing, but simply to rediscover the freedom of action that's indispensable to our happiness.

Hanami and Momijigari: the link to nature

The Japanese are very attached to nature. They respect and venerate it, and visit the countryside regularly to benefit from the changes of season. There are two main festivals honouring nature in Japan: *Hanami*, in spring, celebrates the cherry blossom; *Momijigari*, the hunt for red leaves in autumn, lets people revel in landscapes transformed by the changing colours of the leaves. Nature is superb in Japan, but she does have the advantage of being universal. Everywhere in the world, but also in your own backyard, you can appreciate the beauty of seasonal transformations, the delicacy of a flower, and the surprising strength of a one-hundred-year-old tree.

Returning to nature helps us reconnect with ourselves. Observing flowers, trees and birds sends us into a meditative state that allows us to let go of thought and live in the present moment. Each week, give yourself a personal mini-*Hanami* or *Momijigari*, depending on the season, and thank nature for her beauty and her blessings. Celebrate her simply by walking with pleasure and curiosity.

Let's play a little

Theory is all very nice, but nothing beats experience. Here are seven challenges, one for each day of your first week of searching, that will allow you to rediscover the feelings in your body, to re-establish a dialogue with – and to be more attentive to – your own needs. A warning: some of these games are more time-consuming than others, so don't necessarily do them in order, and adapt them to your schedule. At the same time, try to complete each one before moving to the next – it's not enough just to read them; they're not magic! To find your *ikigai*, you must spring into action.

Challenge
Holiday straight away

Rest assured, it's really not about taking three days or even a single day off: rather, it's a question of attitude. Tomorrow, whether or not it's the weekend, or whether or not you're working, you'll act as if you're on holiday. I can see you coming back at me with your constraints and other obligations. No problem – we're keeping those constraints and obligations. We're just changing the way we approach them.

• Get up half an hour earlier than necessary so you can take time to do something that really brings you lots of pleasure: take a bath, do a few yoga poses, eat breakfast in bed, read a book or the newspaper, savour a good cup of tea. The objective is to begin the day with thirty minutes of pure happiness you've decided on the night before so that you're organised and ready: have the good book within reach, have on hand what you need to make a fantastic breakfast, have some luscious bath oils at the ready. That way, you'll optimise your experience.

• The moment you get up, just before your magical thirty minutes, think of what you've prepared and about this little time of pleasure you're giving yourself. Rejoice in this moment in advance with a huge smile.

● Do each thing in your day as if you were doing it for the first time. If you have to go shopping, rediscover the shops in your local area, imagining the things you would buy if you weren't in your own neighbourhood. If you go to work, take a way you've never taken before; on the way, go into that little gallery that catches your eye. At lunch, give yourself a coffee break with a book.

● If you're working today, approach everything from a new angle, as if you've never been in that place before. Have a coffee from the machine that you've never tried. Do the opposite of what you'd normally do: give a warm greeting to the nasty receptionist who – you're sure – hates you; reorganise your desk as if you're preparing it for someone else; make that phone call you didn't make last week; experiment with new things, trusting your intuition.

● Do at least one thing in a spontaneous way without holding yourself back. Devour that chocolate tart; snap up that seat on the terrace to enjoy a lovely cocktail; give yourself pleasure without thought or restraint – yes, the cocktails are pricey in that bar, but they look so good! Yes, a chocolate tart can be unhealthy, but not today! Let go of all those negative thoughts and savour it.

● In the evening, before you go to bed, note down the three best moments of your day, then note how you feel: light, sad, joyful, calm ...?

● If you loved this day, make a list of the very serious reasons that prevent you from doing these things every day. Cross out the three worst ones. What's left? What's keeping you from everyday joie de vivre? Is it an idea you should break away from?

This experience allows you, above all, to understand that living a lighter, more joyous life in accordance with your desires is completely accessible, and indeed easy, without making any major changes, apart from a subtle one to your attitude.

Game

Rediscover the pleasure of walking

Walking: you do it every day. But what does walking really involve? How do you balance your feet? Do you put more weight on one side than the other? You have no idea, and yet you walk all the time. It's become so automatic that you don't think about it anymore. Let's play at no longer being automatons. Follow this guide.

● At home, when you have five minutes to spare, walk in bare feet. Gently assess every movement without changing your gait, just noting what happens. Do you have the impression that your right foot is heavier than your left? Do you place your heel with the same rhythm on both sides? Note each tiny detail. Which part of your foot touches the ground? Is the sensation the same on both sides? Then take note of the external elements: is the air hot, cold, freezing, gentle, harsh ...? Bravo, you just learnt to walk consciously! Easy, right?

● The next time you have to go somewhere, walk there. You're going too far to walk the whole way on foot? Get off the train three stations earlier, park further away, whatever you have to do to walk for ten minutes. For half of it, do as you did at home and walk normally, but consciously. Just for the pleasure of connecting with all those forgotten sensations.

● When you return home in the evening, thank your feet for carrying you all day and give them a little massage with a neutral vegetable oil and a few drops of a favourite essential oil (vanilla, lavender, chamomile, orange blossom ...). It's an excellent way to gently reconnect with your body, through the simple pleasure of a pleasant ritual to mark your passage from outside to inside.

That's how, with a few short minutes of attention, you can make contact once more with your forgotten feelings. Very little effort, lots of wellbeing.

Magic
No more chores

You have to wash up? Make dinner? Then rejoice, for you're about to experience an exceptional moment. We generally despise those small daily acts we call 'chores'. We curse the existence that obliges us to devote ourselves to these activities rather than lounging around in the bath or playing Mario Kart. But since these activities are part of life, hating them only serves to make your existence unpleasant. What if you tried to appreciate them? Here's a little game that will allow you to change your point of view. Let's take doing the dishes as an example, but you could do this with any chore at all. Today, you're going to do the dishes for the first time in your life, step by step. Here's how you go about it, being aware that you can adapt each suggestion to your own tastes and your own rhythm. The only imperative: take pleasure in it. It's up to you.

● **Run the water,** appreciating the fact that you have running water at all – it's quite practical, really.

● **Feel the water running over your hands;** the sweet sensation of rolling water.

● **Add a few drops of detergent;** sniff and note how good it smells. It doesn't smell good? Tomorrow, buy real liquid soap and the essential oil of your choice (peppermint, lemon …). Use a scent you love.

● **Take note of the effectiveness of your gestures,** how rapidly the dirtiness disappears.

● **Appreciate how clean and impressive** that pile of dishes is.

● **See how pleasing it is to have a completely clean kitchen and beautiful, neat crockery.**

Did you find pleasure in it, even if only a little bit?

Each moment of your daily life should bring you a maximum of satisfaction. Each action is a choice. There's no such thing as a chore: that's a biased way of seeing things. No one's making you do the dishes. You have to do them? No, you choose to live in cleanliness. You make the choice to eat from pretty plates when you could eat from disposable plates, or go to a restaurant, or throw out dirty dishes and buy new ones. You decided to do the dishes because it's more economical, better for the environment, easier for you. It's your choice. Yippee!

Mini-test

The great square of chocolate

Have you ever savoured a square of chocolate? I mean really. While letting it melt. While appreciating it in all its dimensions. This is your job for today. Hard, eh? Here's how:

● **Start by buying a real block of chocolate,** from a real chocolatier. Yes, it will be a bit more expensive – although not always. But it's important to have really good-quality chocolate for this discovery. Buy your preferred type: dark, milk, hazelnut, it doesn't really matter, as long as it makes you salivate in advance.

● **Think about this chocolate** and how much you want to eat it. Doesn't it look delicious? Try to imagine its taste right down to the smallest details. Visualise the moment when you'll finally be able to taste it.

● **Set yourself up somewhere comfortable** and break a square off the block.

● **Start by looking at it.** What colour is it? Is the colour uniform? Is your mouth watering just looking at it?

● **Smell it.** Try to analyse the aroma, as if you were a wine expert. What do you find within this smell? Toasted hazelnuts? Vanilla? Cherries? Coffee? Close your eyes, concentrate and try to name at least three scents.

● **Place the square on your tongue.** Let it melt gently. Appreciate all the work that went into making it possible for that square of chocolate to reach your mouth. Think of the farmers who cultivated their cocoa plantations, of all the people who were involved from the time the seed was sown to the day when the beans were harvested. Then visualise the path taken by those beans: their roasting, the aromas, the blending. Imagine the chocolatier melting their mixture. Appreciate all the work that has allowed you this divine moment.

● **Return to the sensation on your tongue.** Has the square completely melted? Is the taste still the same as it was at the beginning? How has it evolved? What taste remains in your mouth once the chocolate square is entirely consumed?

Bravo: you just truly tasted chocolate in complete awareness! If you extend this field of consciousness a little to all your different meals, you'll eat less and better, and with greater pleasure. Goodbye diets, hello happiness.

Challenge
What's my body saying that I can't hear?

Today is the day for your body. Plan to do this challenge soon: it must have happened by the end of this week. There's no need to find a free day, but if you're not working, that's even better.

● **Stretch when you wake up.** Like a cat. Take time to stretch each limb gently to wake yourself up completely before you get out of bed.

● **In the shower, rub your body** from head to toe with a loofah mit or a brush. This movement will continue to wake up your body gently.

● **At breakfast, have a fresh fruit or orange juice,** or a multi-fruit smoothie – whatever you feel like, but it must contain fresh fruit.

● **Throughout the day, try to listen** to what your body is saying to you. You're yawning? A rest might be beneficial – five minutes is often enough. Your feet are jumping around all over the place? Go for a walk, even if it's only around the room you're in, but ideally in a nearby garden. Your stomach is rumbling? Go to lunch. Yes, even if it's 11.30. If a shiver runs through you, make yourself a cup of tea or coffee to warm yourself up. In short, be aware of the small signals from your body and try to respond to them in the best possible way given your circumstances.

● **In the evening, rest for a few minutes to think over your day.** What did your body allow you to realise? How did those around you and/or your colleagues experience this change of attitude on your part? In your opinion, could you live like this every day? If your answer is no, what's stopping you?

The aim, of course, is that from now on every day will be a day for your body. Finding your *ikigai* will help to make your life richer, but you must prepare yourself by being in good health and full of energy. And for that, you must take good care of your marvellous machine.

Magic
Marvellous
massage

Book an hour-long massage and get 100 per cent out of that time.

● Make sure you choose a place that allows you to become completely calm and allows time for resting after the treatment.

● During the massage, concentrate on your sensations in the area being massaged. Visualise the movement of the hands of the person massaging you, and try to feel each little zone of your skin and its pleasure.

● As soon as you feel like you're getting lost in your thoughts, return to your sensations, to your pleasure.

Leave the salon having had a huge dose of endorphins, the pleasure hormones, and feeling more alive than ever!

Game

Smile:
it's you who
decides

With this game, you'll be making note of the extent of your power. It will take place in two separate phases.

1. Me, Oscar the Grouch

- This morning, leave your house pouting.
- Be grumpy and hardly say hello.
- Eat lunch in your own corner.
- Look at the floor on the bus, and imagine that all the people around you are uninteresting and stupid.
- Notice how completely the atmosphere is poisoned.

2. Me, joyful

- The next day, leave your house with a wide smile.
- Share this good humour with other people as much as you possibly can: greet every person you meet with a head signal or a small, friendly hello.
- Smile at the bus driver, the baker, the people in the elevator.
- Say something nice to each person you have an exchange with.
- Give compliments to strangers.
- Notice the waves of joy you create.

The idea? To make you understand through experience that you're the boss. It's up to you to decide if your day will be joyful or morose. And when you line up all those days, they'll soon make up a year, a decade, a lifetime. It's you who chooses. All you need to do is take back control.

I'M NOT
WHAT I BUY

In a world that encourages us to try and keep up with inaccessible ideals of beauty and lifestyle – whether its through the glossy photos of Instagram or the envy-inducing words on Twitter and Facebook – it's harder and harder not to cave in and adopt an imaginary identity, that 'ideal me' that allows us to achieve recognition in the short term.

This week, we'll take inspiration from Japanese minimalism to remove you from that false you and lighten your house and soul in order to leave room for you to find your true self again.

If you've never bought something to make yourself feel more important, smarter, more beautiful, richer, more unique, more elegant ... skip this week. **For everyone else, this stage will transform you.**

Let's think a little

For me, minimalism began when I went away on holiday. My conversion from fashion slave with an overflowing wardrobe to minimalist convert occurred when I was in India. I left on a three-month trip and was travelling by motorbike. It was therefore necessary to travel light and to stick to a strict minimum. In my wardrobe at home were a little over one hundred pairs of shoes, about thirty pairs of jeans, around fifty tops, I don't know how many dresses, dozens of bags, jewellery and other accessories. In my backpack: a pair of jeans, a long skirt, three T-shirts, three pairs of underpants, a toothbrush, toothpaste, a bar of soap, a hairbrush and two hair elastics. On me: a motorbike helmet, a mini-handbag, a telephone, a credit card, a few rupees, a spoon and a passport. That was all.

The shock of this road trip was to realise that I wasn't lacking anything. I could have lived for the rest of my days like that, without anything more. Not only did I not miss things, but I felt a real freedom. The possibility of moving, of being able to leave a place in ten minutes, gave me a feeling of lightness I'd never felt before. It was a revelation.

The things I told myself back in Paris when shopping for clothes – 'I'll die if I don't get this new dress', 'I need a new pair of jeans', 'Shopping makes me happy' – were nonsense. It was just a way of filling my desperately empty existence. Since that trip, I've had an enormous clean-up, I only occasionally buy new things and I've invested in really beautiful, classic pieces made from natural materials. For me, minimalism isn't deprivation, but a conscious way of selecting desirable, useful and durable objects.

To limit my purchases, I made a rule for myself: if an object came into my home, another had to leave. Given that I now have only things that I love, this has made me very particular.

Aligning my life with my new convictions was quite complex, because shopping wasn't just a pastime, but also my way of earning a crust: I was a fashion photographer and blogger. It was clear that I no longer wanted to put my energy into making people dream about inaccessible fashion items. Did I want to incite others to do what I no longer wished to do myself: buy more and more, desire novelty again and again? At the beginning, I told myself that since I was paying better attention to my choice of brands to collaborate with, I was motivating people to make good choices. That I was advocating quality. That I was letting people dream and this wasn't hurting anyone. But I wasn't completely convinced: I didn't feel quite right in my sparkly boots.

And so I underwent a conversion. Thanks to my new minimalism, I could economise, refuse the jobs that no longer made any sense for me, allow myself the luxury of studying, returning to India to do courses, investing in my own personal development, my life, my future, rather than in the umpteenth pair of perfect jeans. For the first time in my life, I had the feeling that I was really deciding what to do.

What is minimalism?

'Less is more' summarises minimalism in a single phrase. The Japanese understand this well, and more often than not live with a strict minimum. But a strict minimum that is beautiful and durable, buying objects with multiple functions and of good quality.

For Japanese minimalism – *wabi* – each person must content themselves with the essentials: a hut, a tatami mat, a bowl of vegetables, the sound of the rain, the happiness that comes from simple things.

And when something is missing? While we would go and buy it, the Japanese minimalist would apply *kufu*, the art of resourcefulness: using creativity to find a solution with the means at your disposal. *Kufu* is using your imagination to reach a goal without having to acquire anything. The idea is to optimise everything we own already rather than accumulate even more new things. For example, if I need a bedside table, why not create one with a pile of books rather than buy one? Reuse, recycle, repair.

The notion of superfluity is different in each culture and from person to person. The idea here is not to turn you into a true Japanese minimalist. If you deprived yourself too much, you would quickly fall right back into its opposite, excess. It's about drawing inspiration from this idea of limiting ourselves, applying it to our ideas about our own fundamental needs and avoiding unthinking consumption.

Stop accumulating, so that you can find the person you really are behind the consumer. Redefine your priorities by taking a step back from our culture of consumption. Ask yourself the vital question: will this object make my life better or more complicated?

Overconsumption: Why do we do it?

Accumulating to feel we exist: it's hard not to fall into the trap of overconsumption when you're searching for your true identity. We're called upon constantly to prove that we can look like a perfume advertisement: nymph-like, young and sexy for women, seductive and virile for men, demonstrating that we've also read the cultural theories of Roland Barthes, and that we're perfectly happy, well-rounded and, of course, accomplished. And so we buy that golden gown or that dinner suit, which we undoubtedly never wear, for lack of appropriate occasions; that philosophy book we'll never have time to finish; that lipstick in a new colour we didn't have yet; the latest iPad case to show we're at the cutting edge; that anti-wrinkle cream to try to preserve our youthful currency; and those elegant shoes that will perhaps give us, for a time, the confidence we lack.

Identity and dressing

Have you already noticed the influence of an outfit? The days when you find the right ensemble – the clothes that make you feel good, the watch that shows your high calibre, the perfect jewellery – you feel on top of the world. You could conquer the world. At the opposite extreme, on some days you feel inadequate and out of place: it itches, it's askew, it doesn't go, and you're ill at ease, wide of the mark.

This phenomenon goes much further. In your quest for an 'ideal you', you could reach a sort of self-fulfilling prophecy: if I dress like a monk, I'll behave like a monk and people will treat me like a monk. This opens up infinite possibilities. The more diverse your style of dressing, the greater your chance of finding an 'ideal you' who corresponds to who you are every day. And so you consume.

Who do you wish to become? Which sort of 'you' do you want to lean towards? With the infinite choice of brands available, anything is possible. By highlighting one facet or another of your personality, you aspire to transform yourself. This crazy promise creates a certain euphoria.

The ideal me

The limit comes when you go beyond your capacity to play the character you're aiming for.

If you're a size 40, but your ideal you takes a 34, and you buy your outfits based on this ideal you, they'll only fit you once you're slimmer. A lot slimmer. Not tomorrow, then. Or next month. And in six months' time, the season and fashion will have changed. At the time, you don't think about that; you project this magnificent idea of you in a size 34. And you buy it. This is how we end up filling our wardrobes and then resorting to the famous claim 'I have nothing to wear.'

It's the same story when you buy that designer table with the glass top that's so beautiful and so fragile – and you have four children. You project an image of the ideal home with a high-end table, and then in a few minutes there it is, strewn with toys, baby food, scratches and plastic cups, as if you're in your local supermarket catalogue. This purchase doesn't correspond to your reality: it feeds your dream.

The identity void

The other consequence of trying to find your identity through shopping is that you won't look any deeper – you will stop at very superficial results. These distractions hinder the search for your true *ikigai*.

You're attempting to fill the immense interior emptiness you feel by buying things and accumulating them in your cupboards. Of course, this doesn't work, and you fall into an addiction to the ten minutes of happiness and fulfilment after each purchase.

It's hard to avoid this trap as long as you're a bit unsure of yourself. Lack of confidence leads to the belief that we need to be someone else to be 'lovable'. Feeding this someone else with a look/homeware/a car is a bottomless pit. The only way to avoid it is to get to know yourself really well, to escape robot mode, to embody who you truly are, without trying to hide behind someone else.

Minimalist and zero-waste books and websites

Books
L'Art de la simplicité: How To Live More With Less, Dominique Loreau, Orion, 2016
The Life-changing Magic of Tidying Up, Marie Kondo, Vermilion, 2014
Soulful Simplicity: How Living With Less Can Lead to So Much More, Cartney Carver, Tarcher Perigee, 2017
Zero Waste Home, Bea Johnson, Particular Books, 2013
Waste Not, Erin Rhoads, Hardie Grant Books, 2018

Websites
For tips on reducing plastic waste:
www.therogueginger.com
To do better with less:
www.liveforless.com.au
On how to care for yourself *and* the planet:
www.mindbodygreen.com
On how to live with less than 100 things:
www.theminimalists.com

Kufu, leaning towards lightness

If you're finding it hard to struggle alone against a society pushing us towards consumption, you can find support these days from new movements that celebrate frugality.

As in Japanese *kufu*, the 'zero-waste' movement is about recycling and reusing, but also, for example, only buying products without packaging. Without becoming 100 per cent zero waste, you can start by buying your fruit and vegetables loose, then stop buying bottled water. Each step, however tiny, counts – and gradually frees you from the enormous rubbish bin in the kitchen and from the chore of taking out the garbage every day.

Another movement: Japanese-style tidying. In her bestseller *The Life-changing Magic of Tidying Up*, Marie Kondo explains how to sort out your things and keep only 'the things that bring you joy': an idea that benefits us all.

More and more minimalists are giving excellent advice on the internet. These communities can sometimes be a little extreme, but joining them grants the apprentice minimalist access to wholehearted advice and support.

Let's play a little

It's time to put lightness into practice in your cupboards and your shopping, to find the 'being' hiding behind the 'having'.

Game

How many objects do you possess?

A minimalist lives with a hundred objects. How far removed are you from this 'ideal' number? We never take the time to take stock of our possessions, even approximately. The idea of our game for today is to take the time to count everything properly.

• Room by room, count everything you own. Count each item of furniture, each object from the largest to the smallest. Yes, you have to count your underwear. Yes, you have to count your spoons and mugs. This can be very time-consuming, so do it gradually, recording in a notebook everything you've catalogued, as if doing a stocktake for a shop.

• Don't throw anything away. Don't think about the usefulness of your objects. Just note where you are with them.

• Thanks to this tally, you'll realise the sheer quantity of possessions you live with. All those things that you have to organise, maintain, move whenever you move house. What effect does that have on you?

Challenge
Thirty-three items for thirty days

This challenge will perhaps be easier for men than for women …

● Take everything out of your wardrobe: shoes, bags, clothes, coats, jackets, jewellery and accessories.

● Make a pile of all your favourites: everything you like most; the things you'd attempt to take with you if there was a fire.

● From this pile, select, in the amounts you would usually, the items you'd pack to go away for a week. Three tops, two pairs of jeans and lots of accessories? Seven shirts, seven pairs of jeans, seven pairs of shoes and a few accessories? Fifteen tops, two pairs of pants and lots of shoes?

● Count your selection without counting underwear and lingerie.

If you're not at thirty-three, subtract or add items until you reach that number.

● Remove everything from your cupboard that isn't part of this selection and put it in a suitcase, or in bags on an inaccessible shelf in your cupboard.

● Arrange your thirty-three items in a practical and pleasing way.

Live for a month with these thirty-three items, not one more, not one less – don't cheat.

The idea is for you to realise to what degree you can spend a completely pleasant day with only these thirty-three favourite items. You'll also see what you miss most, and what, strangely enough, don't miss at all. After this, sorting, emptying, and saving space will scare you less.

Magic
Imaginary purchase

You see something in a shop you really want. The little exercise over the page will allow you to let go of that impulsive desire to buy as easily as breathing out. Let's take as our example a pair of shoes, but this works for anything. For the optimum effect, take lots of time to experience each step, visualising it in detail and calling on all your senses.

● Imagine this pair of shoes on your feet. They're beautiful. They smell lovely and new.

- Now see yourself wearing them. Everyone is giving you compliments.
- You wear them all the time. They don't even hurt your feet anymore.
- You see yourself in them at work. Everyone is admiring you in your new shoes.
- You see yourself in lots of situations, always wearing your superb shoes.
- They're starting to develop little creases, but they're still really beautiful.
- Little by little, your desire to wear them declines. You alternate them with other pairs you already have and that you love too.
- They start to wear out and are looking old. You're a bit embarrassed about them.
- You wear them less and less. They very often stay in the wardrobe.
- They are less and less attractive.
- Your shoes no longer have any charm. You give up wearing them altogether.
- You see your shoes sorted into the 'throw away' pile.

If you've played this game properly, you'll no longer have any desire at all to purchase this sudden new love.

Challenge
Zero purchases for seven days

Living without consuming, making the most of time as it passes, freeing yourself to make room for reflection, pleasure and meditation. This challenge is about you living for seven days without buying anything. Or getting someone else to buy it for you, of course.

- Content yourself with whatever you have to eat in your cupboards and the fridge. Plan all your meals for the coming week.
- Prepare homemade salads, sandwiches or small meals for your lunches.
- Bake some biscuits to take with you for snacks.
- Run out of salt? Use soy sauce or spices.

Can't live without it? Ask your neighbours to give you some.

● Trouble with your scented candles? Get out your essential oils.

● No more batteries? Do without the object that requires them for the rest of the week.

In short: get help from other people, borrow, barter, try everything you can to avoid buying anything.

Once the week is over, check in with yourself. What did you really miss? What did this challenge lead you to discover: new contacts, new ideas, savings …? Could you keep it up for longer? Could you go for two or three days each week without buying anything? Without compensating for it on the other days?

Magic
Sorting that

Making space at home allows you to make space within yourself, to bring clarity to your ideas, to make room both literally and figuratively. Let's do it!

● Start with the room that's the most cluttered. Go room by room, even if you have to do it in several sessions.

● Take out everything in your cupboards, on your furniture and under it, and make a big pile in the centre of the room.

● Take one object at a time and ask yourself three questions. Is this object indispensable? Does it make me happy? Does it make my life easier? If you answer 'yes' to at least two out of three of these questions, keep it. If not, get rid of it without regrets. Take care with souvenirs and other objects with sentimental value: you don't need a concert ticket to remember that magic moment any more than you need a hideous mug to evoke your visit to Prague or Los Angeles.

● Separate the discarded objects from those you're keeping, sorting them into bags to sell, throw away, or give to charity, and take them out of the room. Sell, throw, or donate them very quickly.

● Carefully arrange the objects you've decided to keep, finding a good place for each that's practical and aesthetically pleasing. Enjoy the space you've gained and the joy of freedom. Make a commitment to yourself not to clutter it up again straight away.

Game

*When do you
buy things*

This is about spotting what happens when you crack and buy something. Next time you make a purchase, take note of the circumstances. Are you in a good mood or depressed? Is the weather good or bad? Who are you buying for? Is it to bring you or someone else pleasure? Who? What time is it? How has your day been? Note all the details, even those that don't seem important to you.

● Ask yourself the same questions for each of your next fifteen purchases, whatever they are, apart from food and items you use daily, of course. Once you've recorded your fifteen experiences, see if you can find points in common: do you always buy things to bring pleasure to someone in particular? Do you usually buy things when you're depressed and there's bad weather?

● Once you've spotted your consumption habits, ask yourself if you could do things differently. For example, could you find another way to bring someone pleasure than a material gift? Cook for them, make them something, give them an experience ... Could you find another activity that would lift your morale? Playing a sport, knitting, calling a friend ...

● Once you've discovered your trigger for shopping, you'll be better able to master it and will be able to find lots of ideas to reduce the frequency of your less useful purchases.

Game

*Your true
luxury*

What if your true luxury had nothing to do with anything material? This game is about working out what really brings you pleasure, what's really therapeutic for you and can serve as your stop button for impulsive purchases.

● For five days in a row, make a note of your simple little pleasures. Start by making a list of things that make you feel good and that are easy to access – not necessarily free, but doable from time to time. Then gradually add the things that come to you during the next five days: a Thai massage, hugging a tree, reading in the garden, doing crosswords, eating ice cream in the sun, looking at the ocean ...

● Each evening during these five days, recall three moments you loved that day and note them down in a separate list: when your chocolate soufflé was a success, when you had coffee with a friend, when you saw a great film ...

● On the sixth day, examine your two lists and look for any points in common: being in communion with nature, savouring good food ...

● Conclude, from your inquiry, what brings you the greatest pleasure in life, what you need more than a new pair of trainers: having a day at the spa once a month, going to the theatre one night a week, discovering a new restaurant each fortnight ...

● Make the decision to give yourself this pleasure as a reward for not making purchases. For example: you're mad about a mid-priced dress, but you don't buy it. You just credited yourself with that money to do something good for yourself in your own way (see the previous point!).

Finding a genuine way to do something good for yourself is an excellent motive for giving up consumption and starting to understand yourself and show yourself consideration. It's a giant leap towards your *ikigai*.

I'M GIVING UP MY RECEIVED IDEAS

To make sense of your life, you need to make space,
to free your inner self from what you don't really need.

Last week, we lightened your cupboards
and made sense of the way you make purchases.

**This week, we'll try to uncover and challenge what
you think you know about yourself** and about life,
to make space for you just to be.

Let's think a little

B efore I read Marc Isenschmid's excellent book *Wipe the Slate Clean* (Doors of Consciousness, 2013) during a long trip through India, I didn't know that I was full of beliefs. I was unaware how much my world was made up of a whole heap of ideas that weren't mine, from the 'You're hopeless' borrowed from teachers and exhausted parents, to the 'Life is nothing but suffering' borrowed from my grandmother, via the 'You have to earn it, it doesn't just fall out of the sky' of popular belief. When I started thinking properly about it, I couldn't get over how many pieces of 'information' about life I'd internalised, persuaded that they were the absolute truth, never even thinking of questioning them.

I thought that I didn't deserve anything, since you can never try hard enough and, given life is nothing but suffering, what good would it do anyway? It was then that I understood a lot about my way of dealing with things. From the perspective of a spectator, I saw the ways my behaviour had been dictated by these beliefs, and reinforced them in the process. For years, without noticing, I had been practising self-sabotage. Introducing an unemployed journalist friend who is really good at networking – unlike me – to my editor-in-chief right at the moment they are hiring, and missing out on the job. Refusing to launch myself as a blogger on social networks when they're just starting up, and then later becoming the only well-known fashion blogger with so few followers. I always found a way of shooting myself in the foot with these rules, which I believed in the same way some people believe in religion. This revelation allowed me to make a huge advance. I hope it will help you to see more clearly too, and bring you closer to who you really are.

Beliefs:
what are they?

During our childhood, adolescence and even as adults, we internalise reproaches, clichés and ideas about ourselves, about others, about money, about happiness, about life in general. Often these reflections come from people we admire or respect at that moment, and this makes these ideas very powerful. We think they're the truth and we never question them. Even worse, we act in such a way as to prove them right. These beliefs constitute the prism through which we view and approach life. A few examples of such beliefs are: I'm shy, I'm hopeless, I'm clumsy, life is hard, people are nasty, you shouldn't talk to strangers, money doesn't make you happy, people with money must be bad, and so on.

These beliefs bring us nothing positive and prevent us from moving forward: I won't try to go up to others because I'm shy. I won't attempt to succeed because I'm hopeless. I won't try to watch out because I'm clumsy. I won't try too hard because life is hard anyway. I won't open myself up to others because they're nasty and, anyway, you shouldn't talk to strangers. Why try to earn money when it won't make me happy, and on top of that will turn me into a bad person?

You will have seen that the point all these beliefs have in common is that they prevent you from living in your own way. They send you in a direction you didn't choose and dictate your decisions so that you can't intervene.

What are my beliefs?

The main difficulty with beliefs is that they're often unconscious, which means they're not obvious or easy to uncover. They're so deeply entrenched within you that they're among the most basic things we learn, like 'fire burns' – you've never asked yourself if it's really true while putting your hand in to see if it actually burns. To recognise a useful piece of knowledge, the method of analysis is quick: is it scientifically proven? What proofs validate this belief and make it a fact? That fire burns is an incontestable fact. That money doesn't make you happy isn't always true. It's perhaps often true, but it's too random to be a fact.

Uncovering your beliefs by distinguishing them from facts is the first urgent step to take towards starting to free yourself from them. Once you've identified these beliefs, even the most powerful among them will lose their power because you will be able to pay attention to them, begin to question them and avoid practising them so religiously.

If I have the belief 'You shouldn't talk to strangers' and I become conscious of it, the next time I stop myself speaking to a stranger, I'll have the perspective to say to myself: 'Yes, you should. Go and talk to them; it'll be good for your career.' Even if I don't necessarily dare go up to them at that particular moment, my belief will have lost ground. The next time I will go up, and if this stranger turns out to be charming, my experience will have proved to me that I was wrong. I will have taken a big step towards freedom.

There are several paths towards spotting your beliefs. The first, and the most accessible to start with, is automatic writing. This is a fancy way of describing the act of setting ideas down on paper in the order they arise in your mind, without trying to form sentences or thinking first about whether what you're writing makes sense. You'll find an exercise for uncovering your beliefs through automatic writing in the second part of this chapter, but here I'll explain the procedure to you. Since your beliefs are embedded within you at an unconscious level, simply taking pencil and paper and listing them while thinking about it is difficult. It's almost impossible. If you try, you run the risk of quickly finding yourself staring in confusion at a blank page. In contrast, by taking it one subject at a time (money, love life, family, friends, health, work, success, sport, nutrition …) and listing things without letting reflection intervene, many of your beliefs will come out as if by magic. You'll see that it's very easy.

Another option is meditation. This demands too much of the majority of us, although some find it easy – but if you can manage it, you will be rewarded. How does it work? First you have to find the style of meditation that suits you: you can remain sitting cross-legged or you can practise the conscious walking we looked at in the first chapter, observing something such as the flame of a candle or nature; you can keep your eyes closed and visualise a scene or an object; or you can even try to empty your mind by concentrating on your breath or on numbers. Each person must find their own way of doing it. Everyone can do it: as with exercise, you just need to figure out what suits you. Before your meditation session, ask your subconscious, or your soul for those this speaks to, to tell you which beliefs are blocking you at the moment – those that are preventing you from reaching your current goal. During your meditation, however, don't think any more about them – just do what you have to and be in the moment. The beliefs you're ready to leave behind will become apparent to you throughout the day.

The most important thing to understand is that this work won't be achieved through thought, since your beliefs have been accepted by your way of thinking for too long for it to spot them.

How do you
let go of them?

It's not easy to abandon something that has accompanied you for years. The more a belief has had an impact on your choices, the harder it is to banish, because letting it go would imply that you've been mistaken for a very long time. This would be far too annoying for your ego.

Rest assured that, as we have just seen, a belief that's been spotted is already half-neutralised. It's all about remaining very aware of the way you act, and not deceiving yourself.

There are different techniques for reprogramming the brain to let go of certain beliefs. These include neurolinguistic programming (NLP) and hypnosis. You can practise on your own using the exercises in the second part of this chapter, and if that's not enough, you can get help from a specialist.

NLP allows us to reprogram our brain, forcing it to let go of its habitual patterns and create new circuits of reasoning. You can, for example, replace one idea with another, or diminish the importance of an idea, making it tiny and ridiculous. It's a very useful technique when you've identified the source of your problem, and if you're struggling with a crippling, deep-seated belief, NLP can be very effective.

Hypnosis will delve deeper into the subconscious, to the roots of the belief. In a state of total relaxation, a hypnotist will enable you to go back to the day when this idea about life was created. In this way, you clarify the reasons for its appearance and you can let it go while understanding that it was a system you put in place to deal with a particular situation, but it no longer has any value today and it's not applicable to all situations.

Whichever technique you opt for, the result will be very quick. The essential thing is to actually become conscious of all the beliefs that are blocking you, because there can be many. It's rare to sort everything out in one session, even if you could tackle several beliefs at the same time. It will take, whether you work alone or with the help of a professional, five or six sessions at least to really relinquish your beliefs and verify that the beliefs you've cleared away haven't been replaced by other, quite similar ones. For example, 'Money is difficult to earn' could be replaced by 'Money is not for me' or 'Money won't make you happy'. You should record everything on paper, being as honest as possible with yourself.

When we realise that our way of thinking has been hijacked by a whole lot of beliefs that don't belong to us, we can find it disturbing. This is normal. Over the years that we've been thinking life is hard, we've done everything to verify it every day in order to remain faithful to it, and then everything is suddenly called into question. What should we believe in? Well, nothing for the moment – for as long as possible, try to stick to just facts.

Furo, the Japanese bath as a purifying ritual for the soul

In Japan, the bathing ritual, *furo*, is very important.[1] At home or at the public baths, *sentō*, each person comes to purify the body, and, more importantly, the soul. Traditionally, people bathe before dinner so that they don't bring the day's worries to the table. They wash before entering the water and rinse off afterwards. The bath should last for a while. They take their time. It's a contemplative pleasure. The heat of the water, between 42 and 55°C, brings about immediate relaxation; the body lets go and the soul follows. When someone dies, once the funeral is over, the family members take a bath to purify themselves and detach from the soul that has departed. Do the same with your beliefs. Let them go with a Japanese-style purifying bath.

1. Japanese bathing should be avoided if you have heart problems or you're pregnant.

Let's play a little

Nothing beats practice for clearing out your beliefs effectively. Here are some ways to identify them, become conscious of them and then put them in their place – so you can open yourself up to a life that better reflects who you are.

Game

Discover your beliefs with automatic writing

Set yourself up comfortably in a place where you won't be disturbed. Take a pen that works well and your notebook.

• Start by closing your eyes and concentrating on your breathing. Count down from ten to zero, breathing in with each number: ten, inhale, exhale, nine, inhale, exhale, eight ... and so on. At zero, open your eyes and make a list of ten words starting with this one: star. Without thinking, list only those words that come to you.

• Now write your first thematic list of beliefs, choosing your theme from the following list: love, money, family, health, work, success, friends, what defines me, what defines my life. Write just the word or phrase, then list in the same way everything that comes to you on the subject, all the little phrases you say to yourself. For example, for work:

Work is healthy.

You need to work hard to succeed.

It's impossible to earn a good living from a job you love.

Work is necessarily tedious: if it's pleasant, it's a hobby.

Work is very tiring, and so on.

• Then do the same for love:

Love lasts for three years.

Men always end up cheating on their wives.

You can never be happy in love in the long term.

It's better to be single than poorly matched, and so on.

● With what defines you:

I'm hopeless at maths.

I'm shy.

I'm jinxed.

I'm useless.

I'm lazy, et cetera.

● And so on for each theme.

Once you've finished, go over each of the themes and add anything that seems pertinent to you. If you have very few items in your list, don't panic. Continue with your week and return to your list from time to time when your brain is less active, such as in the morning just after waking or in the evening just before bed.

You now know which beliefs you're ready to leave behind. There are of course lots of others, but these are the ones that have allowed you to become conscious of them. Once you've put an end to them using the challenges and games that follow, you can return to this exercise to find more.

Challenge
Positive affirmations

Choose from the beliefs you just uncovered the three that weigh you down the most: those that are stopping you from moving forward in your life.

● This challenge is about finding a positive affirmation that will neutralise each of these beliefs. Note that it's not about finding its opposite, but about establishing a fairer phrase, one that's closer to your truth and that puts this belief in its place: consigned to oblivion. For each belief, you will ask yourself three questions: When is this statement false? How could I reformulate it to bring it into closer alignment with the truth? How could I turn it around to make a positive formulation of it?

For example, take the belief 'I'm shy.' Let's move on to the questions.

When is this statement false?

At work, I manage to overcome this shyness and make presentations in front of several people.

How could I reformulate this statement to bring it into closer alignment with the truth?
Sometimes I'm afraid of talking to people I don't know.
How could I turn this statement around to make a positive formulation of it?
I'm more at ease with people I know.

As another example, take the belief 'Love lasts for three years.'
When is this statement false?
My friend Regina has been with her husband for twelve years, and they're still very much in love.
How could I reformulate this statement to bring it into closer alignment with the truth?
Love can sometimes end after three years of a relationship.
How could I turn this statement around to make a positive formulation of it?
Lots of couples that have been together for many years are still very much in love.

Once you've defined your positive affirmations, check to see if they speak to you. They must seem true, logical and fair. If they don't, don't hesitate to reformulate them until you've found the most suitable wording.
This exercise will allow you to put your beliefs into perspective, to weaken them and find a new formulation that suits you better, that is closer to your own experience and your vision of life. It's one step closer to your true self; one step closer to your *ikigai*.

Magic

Cleaning out the library of ideas

Get a friend or friends to read the hypnosis visualisation below to you, or alternatively you could record it on your smartphone to listen to peacefully at a later time. Find a very quiet place away from any distraction, set yourself up comfortably and request not to be disturbed by anyone for the next half-hour.

• Lie down and relax. Take off any clothes or accessories that impede your relaxation. Now play back your recording of the text below or ask your chosen person to start reading it.

Let go of any tension. Put your day-to-day worries aside. You're here to take care of yourself, to do good for yourself. Take three big breaths, deep lungfuls of air. Then choose a colour. With each breath, this colour will gently start to move into you. At first at the surface of your skin, then your feet, then rising gently up to your thighs, then your hips, your waist ... Then, the inside of your body will also change colour, each organ: your intestines, your stomach, your lungs, your heart ... With each inhale, allow yourself to feel the benefits of this colour washing through you. With each exhale, push everything that doesn't serve you far away.

In front of you is a staircase. You decide to use it to descend. Down, down, down you go. It seems like you descend forever, and while you descend, you let go of all those tensions, all those doubts, all those received ideas. You descend confidently, further and further. Right at the bottom of the staircase, when you've finished your descent, you see a path. Move towards it at your own pace, letting go, not trying to see the path straight away, just continuing to make your way down.

Take the path and make your way along it slowly, taking plenty of time to let the atmosphere wash over you. What can you hear? What can you see? What can you smell? Are there things you can touch? Taste?

You continue along this path, and at some point, a little bit further on, you'll find a house. Move towards it slowly, making the most of everything that's offered to you along the way.

Now you're standing in front of the house. Push on the door and enter. Take the next door inside that seems the most welcoming to you.

You find yourself in a room, a cosy place that corresponds exactly to what you love, with an atmosphere you like and pleasing decor. A fire is burning in the hearth and the wood is crackling gently. You lift your eyes to the wall and you see you're in a really beautiful library full of old books.

Take time to observe and notice that, as in all libraries, the shelves are labelled with themes. One of the shelves has your name on it. Take out all the books on that shelf and destroy them using the method of your choice: you can tear them up, throw them into the fireplace, feed them to the lion sitting on a cushion near the fire … use the image that speaks to you the most. Then do the same with each of these themes: money, health, life, love, people, friendship, success … Do the same even with the books on the unnamed shelves. Leave nothing behind. Once you've completed your mission, rest in the garden, drinking a glass of water or a cup of herbal tea and observing nature, then gently, at your own pace, return to the here and now.

This visualisation has the advantage of accelerating the process of distancing yourself from your beliefs, even from those you're not yet conscious of. You can make use of this accelerator as often as you need over several weeks, then once every season for a regular clean-out.

Game

Drawing multiple projections

Like our own beliefs, there are the beliefs other people project onto us, and what we imagine other people think about us. These amount to a lot of pressure we put on ourselves unnecessarily.

• Take a piece of paper and a pencil. Draw yourself in the centre of the page.

• Draw onto yourself all the attributes of each project or profession that other people hoped/imagined for you/that you hoped for yourself. For example, if you think your mother would have liked you to listen more, draw yourself a big ear; if your father hoped you'd become a doctor, put yourself in a white coat; if you were often treated like the class clown, draw yourself with a red nose; if you used to want to be richer, draw a wad of banknotes in your hand; if people often used to say that you had a beautiful voice and you could be a singer, add a microphone, and so on.

● Look at this image representing what you believe you should be. Note the fact that it's impossible for you to fulfil all of these demands at the same time, especially as they're sometimes contradictory. Then destroy this drawing in the way that pleases you most (burning it, tearing it up, screwing it into a ball, dissolving it in water …), forcefully letting go of all these expectations.

Bravo! You just cleared a little more space to make room for the person you really are.

Challenge
The opposing view

Take a belief that's still blocking you. Choose it carefully, because you're going to live with it for the whole day.

● With the first person you bump into, state your belief and watch your listener's reaction. You might say, for example: 'You know, Isabel, money doesn't make you happy.'

● At your coffee break, express your belief as a question and put it to all the people there. For example, 'Do you think money makes you happy?' and note what's said.

● At lunchtime, take a different tack with the people you're eating with: 'Money makes you happy, I'm certain of it', and observe their reactions.

● That evening, take stock of what was said. Note that everybody has an opinion on the subject.

● Who was the most convincing? Do you still have the same thoughts about the subject? What's changed? Why?

Confronting a belief with the opposite idea puts it into perspective: it's an opinion just like any other. By taking the mystery out of the idea, we make it harmless – it's just your opinion, not your religion.

Game

*Acting
as if*

Take a belief about yourself that seems utterly unwavering – one that's so strong you doubt you could give it up for one day, you're so convinced that it's the truth. Today, you're going to decide to live as if you believe exactly the opposite. Just for twenty-four hours.

• Find the exact opposite of your belief. For example, 'I'm shy' becomes 'I'm a real extrovert'; 'I'm hopeless' becomes 'I'm awesome'; 'I'm stupid' becomes 'I'm super-smart'; 'I'm clumsy' becomes 'I'm very skilful.'

• When you wake up, take a few minutes to completely embody your character. Visualise yourself and imagine what your day could be like.

• Ask yourself a few practical questions: How would someone who's really sociable behave in the office? How would someone who's awesome manage their workload? How would someone who's very skilful go about their workday?

• With each micro-choice of your day, do what your character would do, leaving all your reflexes and habits behind, even the simplest of them, and questioning everything: shower or bath, bus or bike, drinks or the movies?

• At each moment during the day, activate responses that are opposite to those that would naturally be your own: stop apologising all the time, don't pay particular attention to fragile objects, and so on.

• In the evening when you go to bed, take stock of your day. What about it was pleasant? What was more difficult? What new habits would you like to develop?

Distancing yourself from your personality, which is defined by your beliefs, allows you to experiment with another world – a forbidden world that opens up thousands of possibilities. Don't hesitate to repeat this little game with other beliefs to free yourself even more.

Magic
NLP screen

Seeing what remains of your beliefs disappear like magic: does that tempt you? Take a deep-seated belief and launch yourself into this visualisation. You can, as with the self-hypnosis earlier, record it and listen to it, but this isn't absolutely necessary. You can also read the exercise through to the end and then start.

● Start by finding the positive affirmation that's the opposite of your belief, as you did in the positive affirmation challenge (exercise 2, page 51). Return to your three questions: When is this statement false? How could I reformulate it to bring it into closer alignment with the truth? How could I turn it around to make a positive formulation of it? For example, 'I'm hopeless' becomes 'I don't always succeed at everything', then 'I do sometimes succeed and I'm proud of that.'

● Close your eyes and imagine a large black-and-white screen where a character is affirming your belief: '[Insert your first name] is rubbish.' Little by little the screen shrinks, the voice becomes twangy, then sharp, then very quickly ridiculous. The screen shrinks again to the size of a postage stamp and then it disappears. The voice becomes more and more distant and fast, incomprehensible. Behind you, on a large colour screen, a character that looks like you is standing at a podium and proclaiming: '[Insert your first name] doesn't always succeed at everything.' Enter the screen, take their place on the podium and proclaim your positive affirmation in a loud voice as if you're delivering a political message: 'I do sometimes succeed and I'm proud of that.' Proclaim this sentence several times in a loud voice until you've really convinced yourself.

This method allows you to reprogram your brain, leaving aside old information (black and white), as distant and ridiculous as the voice that announces it, and replacing it with your new way of seeing things. You can repeat this exercise with other beliefs.

I'M NOT WHO YOU THINK I AM

We often believe we know ourselves. We think we're heading in the right direction, then life suddenly pulls us back in line with a setback, an accident or simply when we're reading something that triggers a realisation.

Here is this week's idea: to become aware of your masks; the performances that hide the real you, even from yourself; the characters you create for yourself depending on the situation; the paths you take that aren't really yours. Deconstruct them to retain only the inner substance.

Let's think a little

or a long time, I believed I loved fashion. For years, I wanted to belong to that pretty and glittering microcosm. I fought tooth and nail to get in and I made it. I moved from health journalist to fashion blogger. I climbed the ladder, succeeding at getting myself known, at getting noticed by designers and brands, at being followed by hundreds and then thousands of readers, at being invited to fashion shows and very exclusive parties. Through my blog, I travelled the world following fashion weeks. I was invited into palaces to take photos and to test new products for major brands. On paper it was a dream job, but in reality, as far as I was concerned, it was lacking.

I was at the Cannes Festival when I realised that none of this really suited me. I realised that this choice wasn't really mine, that it had been motivated by poor reasons: to please my father, who admires artists; to please my mother, who loves fashion; to please everyone, because so many people dream of being a part of that world.

I'd been invited to Cannes under excellent conditions. The most prestigious brands had done my hair and make-up and dressed me, and I was on the guest list for all the VIP parties. I had one job: to make my readers fantasise by telling them about my daily adventures there.

But I didn't feel like I belonged in this world. In fact, I had the impression that I had nothing to do with it. It was the third night of this masquerade: it was midnight, I had a flute of rosé Champagne in my hand, I was at the most exclusive party being held that day, the bun in my hair was really tight, my dress was scratchy, and my pumps were crushing my toes. I felt like I was in disguise. I tried to smile into the camera lens, but I couldn't do it. It was at that moment that I understood. I'd reached the limit of what this job could offer me and I felt awful. I couldn't even manage to put on a fake smile for a photo, I was so sad at heart. Like Cinderella, I ran from the party – barefoot, otherwise it would have been impossible. After I'd cried for forty-eight hours, I swore to myself that I would change my life radically. None of it made sense and that was the problem. It took me almost a year to find a new direction, and two more to flesh it out. It took courage to abandon my privileges, but today I finally feel like myself, and you can't put a price on that.

False choices

Many of us believe that we make our own choices, when in reality they are determined by criteria that don't even depend on us. For example, when we're choosing a professional direction, we seek to satisfy the desires and hopes – expressed or secret – of our parents and our nearest and dearest; we seek to compensate for a lack of money, prestige or family generosity. We act in the name of what we think we want, whereas if we looked into our true motives, we'd realise quite quickly that very little of our self is invested there. As a consequence, we often find ourselves on paths we think we have chosen, but that in reality don't suit us at all. It's for this reason that, in searching for your *ikigai*, we begin with a good clear-out to make space. After our beliefs, we need to let go of our false ambitions, the false 'me's we construct to please other people, and the pretences we create to keep up appearances.

Who are you?

If you attempt to answer this question, you'll probably give your first name and surname. And yet your parents could just as easily have given you a different first name and you'd still be you all the same. Then you'd perhaps say what your profession is. This will give a vague indication of the socio-professional circles you move in, but even then, we still wouldn't know who you are. Do you know who you are? Have you ever asked yourself the question? What defines you? What are your values? What things do you consider essential? Who do you like to spend time with? What do you love doing? What differentiates you from others? What makes you unique?

Who are you trying to be?

Before you even start asking yourself who you are, it's good to find out what you're not, what you are no longer, what you no longer have any need to be. In transactional analysis in psychotherapy, we say that we're influenced by 'drivers'. These are the orders that we received from our family circle during our childhood and that are still guiding us today, without us realising it. We can count five 'drivers':

Be perfect
Be strong
Try hard
Hurry up
Please others

Be perfect

As a child they were told to be good, to be quiet, to not really be a child, to do everything well, to tidy everything up. Someone under the influence of 'Be perfect' is cautious, thinks things through carefully before making a decision and always tries to do as well as possible, to the point that they forget what's really important.

To free yourself: To come out from behind the mask of perfection, bear in mind that nobody is perfect. And if no one else is, how could you be? Try to remember the last time you did work that wasn't perfect. What were the consequences? Just taking a step back is enough: in discovering your mask, you've already done three-quarters of the work.

Be strong
As a child they were told: 'Don't cry', 'It's not that bad', 'Don't make such a fuss.' They were asked to behave like adults very early on, not to feel sorry for themselves, to look after their brothers and sisters, to be responsible. An adult under the influence of 'Be strong' will be someone who's very active, who carries on without asking questions, who seems able to move mountains. Bulldozer that they are, they'll ignore their own needs and those of others.
To free yourself: Try to remember who asked you to be strong, to be steady, not to show any weakness. And now decide as an adult what you still hope to retain from these recommendations. Force of character? Probably. Tenacity? Yes. Total escape from all fragility? Surely not.

Try hard
They were told so often that they could do better, that they should adapt – that they've forgotten who they really are. They had to work hard at school to deserve being rewarded, they had to push themselves as hard as possible to achieve the level expected – or the level they thought was expected – by the people around them. They are so self-willed and persevering that they work much more than anyone else. But despite all their efforts, they feel like they never do enough. Sometimes they even voluntarily – sometimes unconsciously – make their life more complicated and create obstacles for themselves. They have trouble finishing things because they're more interested in making the effort than achieving the result.
To free yourself: Work at letting go, accepting not being able to do something or not having to always be the one who makes the

effort. Open yourself up to the idea that you deserve it, however it comes to you: that simply by being on Earth you have a right to abundance. Meditate on the fact that nature meets our needs, and not everything requires us to make an effort. Even if you open yourself up to this idea only a little, you're winning.

Hurry up

Throughout their childhood, they were told to go faster: 'Quick, we're going to be late!', 'Go and get dressed, we have to get going!', 'What are you doing now? Hurry!' Time became something to stress about. They're always afraid of wasting their time; they get bored very quickly, jumping from one subject to another, from one activity to the next, in an eternal quest for time. They always want to make the most effective use of their time, but they do so anxiously.

To free yourself: Travel to a country where time is treated differently: where people aren't always in a hurry and the norm isn't to be stressed about being late. By waiting for a train that's eight hours late and watching how the locals sit it out patiently, having a siesta or meditating, you'll find lots of ways to reconcile yourself with boredom.

Please others

As a child, they were shown that what counts is to satisfy other people – to whom they'll always come second if, say, there's one more slice of cake, some time, a seat ... 'Make the people around you happy if you want to be loved' is the message they take in. 'There's no unconditional love here'. It's great to be altruistic, but 'Please others' can go on until you forget who you are completely, which can lead to burnout and depression.

To free yourself: You must reconnect with your own needs and make it a priority to satisfy them for just one day. Then observe how you respond. How do you feel? Do you find it easier to take care of others once your own needs are satisfied?

It's possible that in reading these descriptions of the different 'drivers', you recognise yourself in all of them, because we all make an effort to be accepted in lots of different ways. Even so, one of these tendencies will often be stronger than the others and will take control: this is the one you need to address as a priority.

One technique that can allow you to free yourself from these 'drivers' is to interrogate yourself about the sense of your actions when you do a particular thing. For example, when you're shopping and cooking for your family. Why do you do that? Do you love shopping? Does it give you pleasure to choose good food? Do you love to cook? Are you going to make a dish that you love and that you want to share and pass on? If your answers to these questions aren't largely positive, then why and for whom are you doing it? And don't say to me, 'I don't have a choice', because we always have more options than we think. For example, in this case, we could: delegate; decide that you each take it in turns to do the cooking and/or shopping; decide that on Monday it's pasta with butter, Tuesday a frozen meal, Wednesday takeaway, Thursday you surprise them by making a new dish, Friday you go out to eat, Saturday it's your husband's/wife's/children's/flatmate's/best friend's turn to make dinner and Sunday it's tinned soup with toast. Wouldn't you say that a pizza reheated with love is worth more than cooking a dish that triggers so much negative energy that it brings no one any pleasure? You'll avoid so much resentment. 'You haven't eaten any of it! I've been slaving over a hot stove all day!' will no longer be part of your everyday life. To return to our original question: why do you do it? It's very probable that one of those 'drivers' is urging you on: 'I must please my family/I must sacrifice myself.' Deconstructing it in this way will allow you to free yourself from it without having to visit a therapist.

Wabi-sabi, the beauty of imperfect things

Wabi-sabi is the key concept of Japanese aesthetics. It's about appreciating the imperfection of objects, the effects of aging, the irregularities – an idea far removed from the classical aesthetic traditions of the West.

Wabi evokes solitude, melancholy, simplicity and asymmetry. *Sabi* speaks of alteration over time, of imperfection, of impermanence. It's an aesthetic ideal that allows an appreciation of the simple beauty of things that, by their nature, are imperfect and incomplete. A wall of rough stones, smoothed by time, not painted or arranged, but just as they are. A chipped vase, a well-worn table … it's a beautiful object of very good quality, which – altered by time – takes on even more aesthetic and sentimental value.

Beyond beauty, *wabi-sabi* is a philosophy of life, a certain type of elegance, of respect for nature and for the time that passes. Rather than running after the perfection shown in magazines and wanting to stop the inevitability of time, what if we applied *wabi-sabi* to ourselves and appreciated our little faults and imperfections? The marks of passing time, the errors we've made, the failures we've known? All of that makes up our beauty, so let's not try to hide it anymore.

Taking inspiration from *wabi-sabi*, we can learn to appreciate our own imperfections and limits. Keep this philosophy of respect for objects in mind, and apply it to yourself and to others.

Let's play a little

Let's start from the principle that you're not perfect and that that's a very good thing. For you to adapt this idea and understand its importance, here are a few light-hearted exercises to do, that will bring you step by step towards your true self.

Challenge

Remove the masks

Today you'll go the whole day without protecting yourself. That is, you'll get through the day without pretences, without lies, without beating around the bush, without playing games. Yes, you'll annoy some people; yes, you'll create conflict; yes, you'll pay the price for your freedom, but now is the moment for you to try to be real and true, if only for twenty-four hours.

• When you get out of bed, first visualise your day: truths will be spoken, pretences will be dropped, but everything will go well. See your circle react with happiness to your new way of being, your friends and family smiling, trusting you.

• From the moment you sit down to breakfast, be honest. But be careful: this doesn't mean be nasty. For example, if you don't like the eggs prepared by your partner with love, don't lie by saying: 'I'm not hungry this morning,' but don't attack them with: 'Oh, no, not your awful fatty scrambled eggs again!' Just say what you feel: 'I don't really feel like eating fat this morning. I'd prefer a fruit salad, because I need the vitamins to feel well.'

• At work, if you're working today, do the same. Avoid lying at any cost, without trying to be unkind. 'No thanks, Maria, I'd prefer not to take a coffee break because I need to concentrate on this spreadsheet this morning.'

● When you're at home, say what you feel, what you need, what annoys you … Don't let anything go: be truthful and direct, but always with kindness. Use 'I' rather than 'you', and always explain your requests clearly.

● In the evening, summarise your day in your notebook, to re-read later when you feel the need, noting what you succeeded in saying and the result you got. Did you have a good day overall? Did you succeed in saying what you hoped to? Did you manage to be completely genuine? In your opinion, in what ways did you fail?

Experimenting with saying things out loud is a big step towards the real you. When we dare to express ourselves without seeking to hurt the other person, bearing in mind our own needs just as much as those of the people we're talking to, we gain freedom and truth, without upsetting everyone as we might have feared.

Magic
Conjure your facades

We all, depending on the circumstances and the people we find ourselves with, have various attitudes we use to adapt ourselves to what we think certain people expect of us. Today, we're going to identify these characters you've created in order to be accepted, with the intention of neutralising them.

● Throughout the day, observe yourself. Note changes in your voice, in your tone, in your posture, and generally be very attentive to your body.

● Each time you notice a change, make a note of it and analyse the situation. Who are you with? What has changed in your environment? To whom and to what are you adapting yourself?

● Also make a note of the attitudes you take. For example, if you lower your eyes when your boss enters the room, or if you puff out your chest when someone you like arrives at the restaurant. Or, even on the telephone, if you change your voice to be more naïve, cooler, softer, more authoritative …

● In the evening, categorise your various attitudes in your notebook, listing them by type: seductive, submissive, superior, mocking, etc.

• Then, reflect on who it is that is triggering these responses in you: do you want to seduce them? Do you want to submit? Are you scared? Record your observations in your notebook, so that you can come back to them easily.

Becoming conscious of our performances allows us to avoid them when we want to and, as a result, to be more genuine in our relationships with other people. The less you play at submitting, seducing or mocking, the more people will appreciate you, contrary to what you imagine. Even if the people who appreciate you won't necessarily be the same ones who surround you at the moment.

Game
Liar, liar!

Today, you have a lying wildcard. You will, as for your 'Remove the masks' day, completely stop lying. This time, though, you have the right to one lie during the day. Choose your moment well and make sure you use your one and only lie on the right person.

• Only lie once, and take good note of what you lied about and to whom.

• Note, once you've used your wildcard, the moments when you would have liked to have another.

• Note which times you miss, and don't miss, being able to lie.

At the end of the day, examine your notes. Could you go without lying altogether? If not, in which circumstances and with whom is it hardest not to lie?

Challenge
Your truths

Have you always wanted to know what people really think of you? You'll like this challenge, then!

• Send an email out to ten of your closest friends or family, asking them to tell you three important truths about you.

• Explain that it's for an exercise and is quite urgent.

• If five people out of the ten respond, that's more than enough.

• Wait until you have at least four answers before you look at any of them in detail.

● Once you've received your responses, see if there is any commonality in what people have said to you.

● Ask yourself if it seems fair.

● Don't get annoyed or upset, but look for what you can learn from these truths.

Armed with this information, you can now not only put it in perspective but also use it to know more about your inner circle themselves, because often what people see in others is what they don't see in themselves.

Magic

No more faults!

Do you think that you're someone who's full of terrible and crippling faults? Yes, as people have told you since you were a child, you're (delete as necessary): lazy, useless, tiring, narrow-minded, unpleasant, negative, amateurish, and so on. Why don't we take a closer look at these ideas?

● Take your three worst faults. Those that people have reproached you for a lot. Those that weigh you down. Those that are blocking you.

● Examine them one by one and find at least two advantages for each. For example, if you think you're lazy, what benefits can you draw from that? You don't waste your time with useless activities? You optimise your work? You know exactly what you want?

● Translate these advantages into good qualities: efficiency, determination, selectivity. From one fault, you've ended up with three qualities!

● Make sure you don't try just to guess your qualities directly from your faults: always ask yourself 'How does this fault serve me?' first. This question will help you find qualities that truly apply to you.

● If one of your faults poses a problem for you and you don't manage to draw advantages from it, ask someone neutral to help you (an acquaintance is better for this than a colleague or a family member). Realising that there's a hidden side to every fault will make you feel so much lighter. Yes, you are a little bit lazy, but thanks to that you've developed lots of good qualities that more or less balance the equation.

Game

Mirror!

What do you think of your friends? What truths about them would you not dare to say to their face? Are there things about them that you'd choose to improve or change? Take out your imaginary magic wand and let's get to work!

- Make a list of the fifteen people who are closest to you and about whom you'd like to change one or several things.
- For each of these people, list what you'd like to improve but also what you admire the most about them.
- Now take your list, cross out all the names and write your own at the top of the page.
- To what extent do these faults and qualities correspond to you? As we saw in the challenge 'Your truths', what we see in other people often applies to us. If I'd asked you to make a list of your faults and qualities, you wouldn't have listed the same things, but the result is still more or less true. Why? Because we don't always see ourselves clearly, the good parts or the bad.

Challenge

Wabi-sabi yourself

This is about learning to appreciate who you are without trying to change yourself.

- Grab your notebook and a pen – we're going to make a list.
- Without thinking too hard, randomly make a list of everything that people appreciate about you.
- Also list everything that you don't appreciate about yourself; everything about yourself that bothers you.
- Then, re-read this second list and try, point by point, to see what is good and beautiful in what you don't like about yourself.
- For example, if you find yourself clumsy, think of the people around you who are clumsy too and consider their little blunders. Don't these things set off a certain tenderness in you? Could you apply this tenderness to yourself? Another example: if you find yourself too talkative, think of all those dinners that you enlivened,

and all those evenings that would have been dead without you, and appreciate this aspect of your personality.

● In this way, examine each of your 'faults' – each failure, each doubt – and see what you can find in them that's admirable and valued. Don't be ashamed of who you are anymore – you can't hide it. Instead, try to appreciate and highlight it so that others appreciate it too. You'll draw immense relief and great freedom from this process.

BUT WHO AM I REALLY?

This week, I propose leading a genuine inquiry into yourself. For this reason, this chapter will be a bit different. It will have a little less theory and a few more games, because to know yourself, you really need to spend some time exploring the subject.

Reflecting on the essence of what gets you going, what inspires you and what fulfils your needs is to find the foundations of your *ikigai*. Until now, we've been clearing space; now, we'll begin to see your real self appear. Are you ready?

Let's think a little

If you'd asked me, a dozen or so years ago, what I wanted or what my priorities were, I wouldn't have known how to answer. At a restaurant, I would take hours to read and re-read the menu, only to order the same thing as the person who ordered just before me. When there was a discussion at the table, I never gave my opinion, because I had no idea what to think: I found the arguments on both sides equally convincing, and the longer I waited to speak the more lost I became. To tell the truth, I didn't have an opinion on much at all and I never knew what I really wanted. 'Whatever you like' and 'lead the way' were my two favourite phrases.

And yet, deep down, I felt that this wasn't working; that somehow I did have desires and ideas – but that expressing them would have meant taking the risk that someone else would disagree, and I would have to defend a point of view that, when it came down to it, I didn't really care about. And so I lived life like a spectator, through other people. I was convinced that this was because of my personality, that it was just the way I was, and I simply had to be that way. That because I was shy, quiet, in my own world, I was excused from giving my opinion.

So I never tried to understand what I needed. I didn't even think about it. I decided that I was a follower and that if that made me unhappy, surely that was normal, as I was convinced that life was sad anyway.

It was only recently that I came to realise that being a 'follower' wasn't a personality type at all, but simply proof that we don't know ourselves very well. I thought I didn't have any opinions, but in reality I'd never taken the time to understand my own values. I thus had no system of reference to ground myself. I thought I had no genuine desires, when the truth was that I simply didn't know how to listen to myself to find them out. These days, I'm much happier than I was ten years ago, which is why I think that one of the keys to happiness is knowing yourself.

You're self-centred

You will definitely hear this reproach if you talk about your quest to other people. In a world where we need to be doing something constantly and showing it – usually on social media – we are not encouraged to take time to reflect on ourselves.

In order to see more clearly into yourself, you'll have to step outside of the rat-race. You must break your routine of 'I'm so busy' and accept being a little bored sometimes. It's about taking time. You cannot find your *ikigai* between the commute and shopping at the supermarket while sending a text to organise your Saturday night out. You'll have to press pause, and people will notice.
'Aren't your coming out with us anymore?'
'Go on, come and have just one drink – you're no fun.'
'Where were you yesterday?'

Wait and see what people ask you to show an interest in. Know that you're not at all obliged to justify yourself, and even less to talk about your progress – that's very personal, and doing so could hold you back. Imagine that you've been talking to your colleagues every day about what you've discovered about yourself on your *ikigai* journey, but last night you had a revelation: you have to quit your job. To say that to them in that forum is too premature: you don't know exactly what it is you want yet, you have no idea how you're going to get there, and you could change your mind. Stay discreet, at least at first – let's say at least until week 9.

It's very selfish

So there you are, preferring to spend an afternoon listing your childhood passions rather than helping Ruby move house, having coffee with Josh, who's down at the moment, or going to see a film with Simone, who feels lonely. For most people, it will be hard to take. What? How dare you be more interested in yourself than in fixing other people's problems?

Accept your choice. You need to take time for yourself, the time you should have been given as an adolescent, then as a young adult. Yes, you should have asked yourself these questions a really long time ago, but no one told you how important it was to know your own priorities or desires. They just said: 'Learn, learn, learn, do well at school, do something prestigious or "safe": science, law, languages, IT, management, secretarial work.' No one ever told you to think about it, to take your time. On the contrary. So yes, it's selfish, but it's vital. You need this time out to know who you are. You'll help the others later, and you'll definitely do a better job once you know what you have to offer them.

The quest for self in books

Here are a few good books about getting to know yourself.

The Subtle Art of Not Giving A F*ck, Mark Mason, HarperOne, 2012

Fruits of the Earth, André Gide, Vintage, 2002

Letters to a Young Poet, Rainer Maria Rilke, Penguin, 2012

The Gifts of Imperfection: Let Go of Who You Think You're Supposed to be and Embrace Who You Are, Brené Brown, Hazeldon Publishing, 2010

Women Who Run with the Wolves, Clarissa Pinkola Estés, Ballantine Books, 1992

The Mindful Day: Practical Ways to Find Focus, Calm, and Joy From Morning to Evening, Laurie Cameron, National Geographic, 2018

What Your Aches and Pains Are Telling You: Cries of the Body, Messages from the Soul, Michel Odoul, Healing Arts Press, 2018

Niwakizendo, the mirror garden

For the Japanese, the garden is like a mirror of the interior life. This is why many create or maintain either a mini zen garden – you know, those little trays of sand that you rake into lovely waves – or a bonsai, one of those little trees in a pot that you can have in a living room. Those who are lucky enough to have a real garden practise *niwakizendō*. This technique of pruning trees is a truly artistic and philosophical exercise that goes beyond shaping the branches into little waves.

The idea of *niwakizendō* consists of the idea that when you prune a tree, you must reveal its personality. Say who it is with the secateurs. By removing branches and leaves, you also make it look older, since old trees have lost branches and foliage through the passage of time and bad weather, making them sparser. It is as if you have made the tree grow up before its time.

By sculpting a tree into this natural design, the aim of this art is to achieve the quintessence of beauty that comes with maturity. It is practised not only by professional Japanese gardeners but also by many amateurs in both Japan and elsewhere in the world.

Pruning is also a form of meditation, of being present during the process in silence and calm. Find your interior peace, but also the childish joy of creativity; be in contact with your interior world and take pleasure in touch and action.

Let's play a little

The aim of this week is to get to know yourself better: we're going to delve into your past and into your ideals to find your true values, your ambitions and what motivates you – an essential step towards discovering your *ikigai*.

Challenge
Return to childhood

As a child, you occupied yourself much more effectively than you do now. What did you do? What was your favourite activity? The one that always made time fly by? Today, you're going to take it up again.

● Don't choose an activity that seems entertaining to you these days, make sure it's really the one you loved from your childhood.

● If the activity from your childhood is still an important part of your life (if it has become your profession or main hobby), try to find another one, in order to gain the full benefits of this exercise.

● If you used to draw all the time but you don't know how to draw now, that doesn't matter. Grab a piece of paper and a pencil, and get drawing anyway.

● If you used to play soccer and you moved to tennis, or even to philosophy, no problem. Go back to soccer for a day, just to relive those feelings.

● Today, spend as much time as you possibly can doing this activity. If it's not something you can keep doing all day, you can do related things: watch a show about it or read a magazine on the subject.

● Make a note of how you feel. Are you uncomfortable? Do you feel ridiculous? Or, on the contrary, have you taken it up again like it was only yesterday? Are you having fun?

● In the evening, think about your day and take stock. Did you have a good time? Why?

● If you didn't enjoy it or you were really uncomfortable, try to work out why you liked it as a child, and what your reasons were for finding the activity fun then.

● If you used to love crocheting because it took great concentration, think about what you do today that requires that same degree of concentration. If you still find pleasure in concentrating, try to expand the number of activities you do that bring concentration into play. If you no longer enjoy it, try to find what you've replaced it with, to understand how the attraction of concentration has disappeared from your life.

Either way, whether you find the activity fun again or not at all, you've revived part of your childhood and rediscovered needs and desires that are perhaps still there, albeit often in other guises.

Game

Revolt!

Today, we're going to look into what revolts you, to understand your system of values and your priorities.

● List five things that you find revolting in the modern world.

● Be as precise as possible.

● Really think about what makes you sick, makes you want to break stuff ... the things that could spur you to action, get you riled up!

● Behind each of your revolting things, find the main values that they violate: justice, liberty, peace ...

● Examine your list of values. Is there one that recurs? Several?

These are your main values, the lenses through which you see your life. But do you yourself really respect them?

Discovering your values and realising that you sometimes don't value them yourself will allow you to replace them with other things, to re-examine your priorities and to understand why you feel so bad in certain situations.

Magic
Your dream job hides a secret

This isn't about working out which potential profession you dream about. Quite the contrary.

- List five professions you would have liked to take up in another life, the ones that you dream about, but that, for obvious reasons, aren't meant for this particular life.
- Take those that seem the most improbable (principal dancer, tightrope walker, top model, singer ...).
- The more ridiculous or embarrassing you find it, the more interesting it is – don't censor yourself.
- Once you have your five professions, make a list beside each one of the qualities that, according to you, are indispensable for carrying them out. Warning: don't list learned skills here, but real qualities. For example, for principal dancer, we would stick to rigour rather than physical fitness, creativity rather than confidence, discipline rather than technique.
- Examine each closely, but in terms of what you imagine rather than the reality of the profession and whether you know about it or not. What matters is your projection: what you invest it with.
- Examine this list of qualities. Do they remind you of someone?
- Re-read your list while accepting the idea that these are the qualities you already have and that you'd like to develop even more. If I'd asked you to list your qualities, these would probably not have been the ones that came to mind. And yet they are your assets. Be conscious of them and tame them – you need them!

Challenge
Be joyful

Today is your official day of joy. Your only obligation today is to be joyful.

- When you wake up, rejoice that it's such a beautiful day.
- Skip down the street on your way to work: joy demands physical expression.
- Smile at everyone, and you'll see that people will almost always smile back.
- Find the most joyful way to complete your tasks for the day: do the shopping in disguise, reply to your emails using words chosen

at random … find a way to play, especially with things that are supposed to be serious.

- Savour each little victory, each little pleasure.
- Express your joy: clap your hands, raise your arms, skip, dance.
- If you find yourself feeling sad, melancholy or depressed, act as if you're really contented: change your body language, lift your chin up, sit or stand up straight, smile. After a few painful minutes of pretending, you'll rediscover your joy.

Finding the keys to your enthusiasm, discovering what makes you joyful and seeing that, when all is said and done, states of sadness are easily transformable without much effort – these are the most accessible paths to your true self. Knowing what made you able to pass from sadness to joy – being aware of your own inner resources – is essential.

Magic
You meet an animal

According to shamans, we all have a spirit animal that helps us and accompanies us throughout our lives. Other animals can also appear in our dreams or our lives to accompany us for a certain time or experience. Here's a little meditation to help you find your own spirit animal.

- Make yourself comfortable in a quiet place where you won't be disturbed.
- Record the meditation over the page on your smartphone, reading in a clear voice, then listen to it calmly.
- As you listen, take ten big, deep breaths. With each inhale, allow your belly to expand. With each exhale, expel as much air as possible.

Close your eyes and walk down a beautiful path.

At the end of this path is an idyllic place. It's a lovely, comfortable place, where you feel great. It can be inside or outside, beside the sea, in the middle of the forest, on a mountain, or a mixture of all three – it's up to you to decide. The temperature is just right, and everything you need to eat and drink is there, all your favourite things. It smells good, it feels nice: everything is absolutely perfect. Make yourself comfortable in the most attractive-looking spot and enjoy the sense of wellbeing that comes from this idyllic place.

An animal appears in front of you. It comes up to you, winks and turns into another animal. This other animal makes an affectionate gesture towards you and, at your touch, turns into a third animal. Thank it and return to your path.

Take three big, deep breaths and slowly return to reality.

● Make a note of the three animals you saw. And without taking time to reflect, make a note of the attributes of each animal: gentle, aggressive, sly, friendly … The first animal you saw represents how you'd like other people to see you. The second animal represents the way that others really see you. The third animal is your spirit animal, the one that accompanies you through your life and represents you on the way. The one you are when you're truly yourself.

When you have a doubt or a question or you need inspiration, you can return to this internal walk, sit down in your favourite spot and ask the question, showing your spirit animal the problem you're struggling with. The solution should appear to you during this encounter or in the days that follow. Pretty useful, right?

Game

Automatic writing

All you need to know is within you. The only challenge is to discover what's hidden at the bottom of your secret sources of shame and doubt.

● Grab your notebook and a pen.

● For each word in the following list, write – spontaneously, without thinking – three other words that they evoke for you. Don't cheat.

● Start by copying each word into your notebook, leaving space after it for your reactions. The list of words is: star, plane, cat, hair, house, artist, feelings, surprising.

● In the same way, answer each of the following questions in three words, without any time for reflection, writing immediately, even if the answer seems absurd to you or completely off-topic.

● Start by copying each question into your notebook, leaving space after it for your three words. What is essential for you? What guides you? What is your mission? What are your assets? What do you want to transmit to the world?

● Re-read your answers. What do they tell you about yourself? Are you surprised by your responses? Do certain ones seem to echo each other in a particular way?

You can use this method, which is often employed in creative meetings, to find the solutions to your worries: ask your question in writing and answer with three spontaneous words. All you need to know is already within you!

Magic
No more
fear

Eek! Are you shaking in your boots? Are you going to run away? What if, on the contrary, exploring your fears could be really interesting?

● List the five things that scare you the most in life. Try to be as specific as possible.

● Relist them in order of importance, from the most dreadful to the least disturbing.

● See if you can group some of them: for example, a fear of death and a fear of the dark are linked in both being fears of the unknown.

● For each group of fears, try to understand the need hidden behind them. A fear of public speaking, for example, means we're afraid of being judged by others, which means we have a need for others' approval. How can we find this approval? By confronting this fear head on and speaking to larger and larger groups of people – from two people at the family dining table to six friends at lunch, to colleagues in the meeting room. Little by little, we fulfil our need and minimise our fear.

Some examples of fears/needs:

Fear of death = fear of the unknown = a need for reassurance.

Fear of emptiness = fear of absence = a need to be surrounded by people.

Fear of flying = fear of losing control of the situation = a need to let go.

Fear of suffering = fear of emotions = a need for self-acceptance.

When you've found the need hiding behind your fear, you won't necessarily know how to fulfil it, but that's no big deal. It's already a very big step towards knowing what you're missing. Well done!

Bonus test

Calling your friends

Today you're going to learn what other people think of you. You'll see that it's much easier than you might imagine.

- List the people around you who you feel close to and who inspire you; who you admire for one reason or another.
- Ring up five of the people closest to you on this list.
- Ask them what they like about you. Suggest to them that they answer spontaneously, without thinking first.
- Then ask them if there's something they envy about you.
- Make an accurate note of what they say, so that you don't twist it around later.
- Compare what each of them said. Were there things that came up more than once? Qualities that lots of them found in you?

There's no greater boost to your self-confidence than hearing compliments and praise from the mouths of those you admire. At the same time, you'll learn which of your qualities are the most pronounced. You have lots of others, but these are the ones that you've started to express to the world.

Bonus game

The secret garden

We each cultivate a secret garden, and yet very few of us have visited it.

- Make yourself comfortable in a quiet place.
- Play yourself the following text – prerecorded on something, like your phone, for example.
- Take ten big, deep breaths. With each inhale, let your belly expand. With each exhale, expel as much air as possible.

Close your eyes and find yourself walking down a lovely path.

At the end of the path you find a large iron gate that opens onto a garden. Enter, greeting the gatekeeper.

At the bottom of the garden, a young girl is playing on the swing and laughing. Go up to her and ask her the secret to happiness.

Listen carefully to her answer and watch her, because she could also answer you in signs and symbols. Thank her and return to your tour of the garden.

You find, even deeper into the garden, a pond. You see your reflection in the water – it's you in the future. Ask your older self how you can help them to have a more pleasant life.

They will answer you either with a phrase, or some words, symbols or gestures. Thank them and continue your visit.

By the time you have enjoyed the beauty of the flowers and smelled their lovely perfume, discovered a herb garden and an orchard, you're ready to leave.

Near the exit, sitting on the steps, is an old man who seems to be waiting for you.

Go up to him and ask him the meaning of life. Listen to and observe his answer, then thank him and say goodbye.

Leave the garden, waving to the gatekeeper, and close the gate. You can return here as often as you wish.

Slowly return to reality, taking three deep breaths and, little by little, moving your hands and feet very gently, then stretching.

Your garden is full of secrets that are waiting to be brought to the surface if you only ask some good questions. What useful things have you learnt about yourself? Don't hesitate to come back.

I'M DIGGING DEEPER

This week, we're going to look at what's going on around you so you can understand yourself better.

What are your interactions with others like?

Where are you at when it comes to the people closest to you?
Your relationships say more about you than you might think.
The quest to find your true self continues – over to you!

Let's think a little

D uring a long trip in India, the aim of which, among other things, was to get to know myself better, I met an amazing girl: Carmen. She was a photographer living in Los Angeles, a true artist who exhibited her work in galleries, sold her photos and made a living from her creativity. She was brilliant, funny and, on top of that, very spiritual: tuned in to meditation, yoga and a connection with the universe. When I met her, I had quite an ambiguous response. On the one hand I felt huge admiration for her, on the other something like terrible hatred. I was annoyed at myself. How could I have the least negative feeling towards this girl who'd done nothing to me? Pushing the darker aspect of my feelings to one side, I got closer to her. I found her magnetic, incredible. The more time I spent with her, the more my admiration grew – but so too did my bitterness. The more I tried to ignore this feeling of jealousy, which I felt was unacceptable, the stronger it became. And yet she was absolutely charming. I had no good reason not to like her. Worse still, she was incredibly generous, both with her time and her money: she invited me to drink tea, gave me a dress, made me laugh, comforted me, took me on various adventures. My first impression should have disappeared. Only admiration should have remained.

Taking a step back from this strange situation, I asked myself what was setting off these negative feelings in me. Rather than trying to chase them away, I decided to face them head on. Then I understood: she was everything I wanted to be, but hadn't allowed myself to be. She was an accomplished artist: I took photos for ads and for fashion websites. She was free and travelled the world alone: I'd never dared to set off on such an adventure. She took a close interest in religion and practised her own form of spirituality: I'd never found my own. She lived in a city that represented success, money and extravagance: I would never have had either the means or the courage to try to live there. She was sweet and kind: I'd always been afraid to show that side of myself, worried by the idea of someone abusing my kindness or thinking I was stupid – 'I don't like to speak ill of her, but she's ... nice.' In short, this negative feeling came from the same root source as my admiration: she did, lived and allowed herself everything I would have liked, but had convinced myself was impossible. She was living proof that you could be creative, talented *and* nice *and* rich *and* successful *and* spiritual. She reminded me that I was putting up barriers for myself that didn't exist. And I found it unbearable.

That day, I understood that it's really interesting to look into the reasons why we find the people who get on our nerves so unbearable. The people we're drawn to or that disgust us have a lot to teach us about ourselves.

Long live jealousy!

Jealousy is a feeling that's frowned upon. We're ashamed of being jealous and we hide it. It's so unacceptable that we even hide it from ourselves. And yet, jealousy gives us indications of what's missing in our lives. It's really revealing. Set aside the negative aspects and use this information: ask yourself what this person allows themselves to do that you don't permit yourself. The people who frustrate you are also good indicators – frustration is often just badly camouflaged jealousy. Why are you jealous? What are the people who frustrate you doing that you're not? Does that girl who all the men find so attractive annoy you? Well, where are you at when it comes to seduction? Does that bloke who talks loudly and makes such huge gestures annoy you? Well, why are you so discreet? Distancing ourselves as much as possible from this violent feeling that makes us want to push a person away is, in fact, a way for our brain to avoid confronting our own shortcomings.

In the same way, jealousy is an excellent indicator of our true desires – and a revealing one. When we analyse these feelings a little, they become a compass. Jealousy is a magical instrument if you know how to use it, you just need to ask yourself the right questions whenever you feel it. What's missing in your life? Which direction should you go in so that you can resemble the person you envy a little more? Be honest with yourself and follow in the footsteps of the people who make you jealous – they'll show you the way to fulfilment.

Goodbye, comparisons

The problem with jealousy is that we're often tempted to compare ourselves with people we envy. This is a terrible trap, because we never have all the facts. Yes, Leila seems super-fulfilled in her relationship, but what efforts is she making each day to achieve that? Is she happy or does she just seem it? Certainly, Charlie is succeeding in his career more than you are, even though you did the same degree, but what's his daily life like? What has he given up? What sacrifices has he made? Even when you have the impression that someone else's life is idyllic, you mustn't let yourself fall into that trap. The reality is often less rosy, and most importantly there's always extra effort behind it that you can't see. Are you ready to put in the same effort yourself?

Comparison is terrible because it devalues you: it makes you feel 'less' or 'more' than someone else, and the result is disastrous. With 'less', of course, we feel devalued, useless, ridiculous. With 'more', we feel threatened, we're afraid the tide will turn and we worry about the future. To avoid all these disagreeable feelings, it's better not to compare yourself at all. It's completely useless. It's just a bad habit you should give up, like smoking. The withdrawal can be painful, but the results are worth it. Put money in a jar every time you compare yourself with someone else. You'll develop the habit of paying attention to it, and you'll do it less and less. With this money, shout yourself a trip abroad, in a culture that can't be compared with yours.

Enough with the scenarios

Michael didn't call you back? He's definitely too busy with his new friend who's going to take your place. Julie isn't here today? She's always sick at the moment, what if she is pregnant? We don't realise it, but we spend our time constructing imaginary scenarios that upset us, creating worries for ourselves when there's nothing to worry about. These scenarios destabilise us for no reason, because more often than not we're completely wrong. Someone didn't call you back? Call them to find out what happened. Someone's snubbed you? Ask why. You'll discover that the reality is much simpler than your fiction!

If you're starting to make a movie plot out of it and you have no means of obtaining a concrete explanation from the person themselves, rather than wandering off into pointless negative fantasies, turn this bad habit into a helping hand towards your future. Train yourself to imagine positives. Mary hasn't called you back? It's because she's preparing a surprise for you. Julian made a face today at the office? It's because you're going to get a raise instead of him. Imagine everything you wish for: if it's not true, it will at least have the merit of making you realise what you want.

Always take the initiative. Yes, it can be a bit embarrassing to ask someone, 'Why didn't you call me back?' but it's less so than inventing an entire story that risks upsetting you or making you pull away from that person. Most of the time, you'll realise that the situation has nothing to do with you.

Wait or ask?

While we're on the subject, you should know that asking is also often the best way of getting what we want. You'd like your husband to take you for weekends away more often? Ask him clearly for just that, don't make hints that only you can understand. You'd love your journalist cousin to help you write your first novel? Get her involved. Don't lose time hoping that one person or another will magically understand your needs and desires. Think about it: if you already have trouble seeing your own needs clearly and you don't ask for them directly yourself, how can you expect anyone else to be able to work them out? People just don't have the time. Do you spend your days asking yourself if this or that person needs your help? Does the fact that she mentioned moving house mean she needs your help? Not really. On the contrary, you appreciate real requests, and the clearer they are, the easier it is for everyone.

What if they say no? Don't turn it into a big drama. Let it go and organise what you need for yourself: surprise *him* with your dream weekend away; sign up for a writing workshop to make progress on your book without putting all the pressure on your cousin.

By asking, you gain a crazy amount of time. You avoid a frustrating and usually pointless wait, and you yourself can quickly deal with all your unsatisfied needs and desires. People will thank you for it.

A few books for daring

For learning how to formulate your demands in the most positive way possible:
Nonviolent Communication: A Language of Life, 3rd edition, Marshall B. Rosenberg, PuddleDancer Press, 2015

For learning how to absorb your doubts:
Daring Greatly, Brené Brown, Gotham Books, 2012

For an example of a woman who dares:
Woman without Fear, J.P. Touzeau, AmazonCrossing, 2015

For daring to say what you think:
Being Genuine: Stop Being Nice, Start Being Real, Thomas d'Ansembourg, PuddleDancer Press, 2007

For emerging from shyness:
Quiet: The Power of Introverts in a World That Can't Stop Talking, Susan Cain, Penguin, 2013

With origami, anything is possible!

For getting to know yourself better, nothing beats meditative activities that allow you to spend time alone with yourself. In Japan, lots of people practise *origami*. It's the art of folding paper, originally intended for making table decorations. It's taught to children at school and it has taken on considerable symbolic importance since it was invented in the sixth century.

Much more than a pastime for well-behaved children, people say that with this practice, anything is possible. This idea comes from the fact that at first it seems impossible to create complex shapes with simple folds, and yet, with perseverance, you always end up getting there. A popular belief even claims that if you manage to make one thousand origami cranes, you'll be able to achieve your dearest wish.

In the windows in some villages, you can see garlands of one thousand cranes of every colour. Symbols of peace, they perform the same function as strings of Tibetan prayer flags. Do you know what you'd wish for if you folded one thousand cranes? Start folding and you'll have plenty of time to think about it!

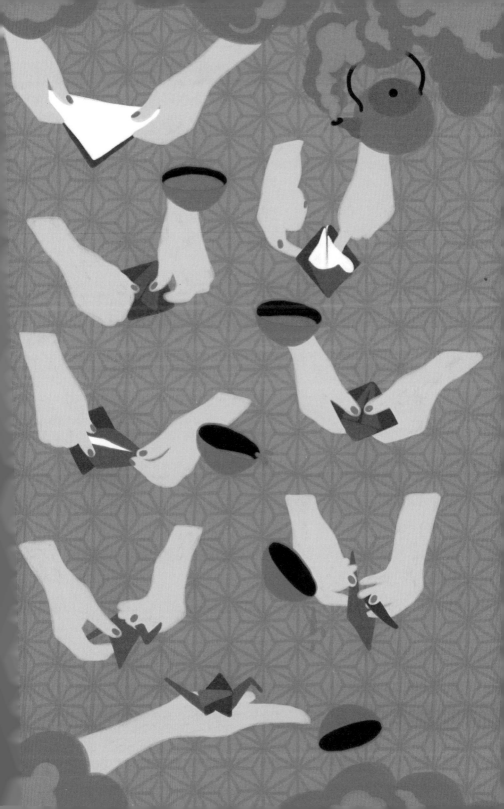

Let's play a little

When we stop making imaginary movies about ourselves and others, we see things much more clearly. Here are a few ways to spot the stories you tell yourself and decipher what they say about you. Have fun by looking into yourself as if you are a stranger – it's more entertaining and more effective.

Bonus game
What do you want?

As we've already seen, knowing who we're envious of can clarify what we really want, so let's dig a little deeper into this idea.

● Make three lists: of the people who make you jealous (don't be ashamed, it's a perfectly normal emotion); the people you envy (the feeling you experience about them will be more positive); and those you admire (no ambiguity here). You'll need at least three people per category for this exercise to work best.

● Beside each name, note three qualities of each person that you'd also like to have. Do this spontaneously, without thinking too much about it first.

● Also note one or two of these people's accomplishments that you dream about – a path you would have liked to follow, a degree you'd like to have done.

● See if certain qualities and pathways come up more than once, or follow a logical pattern.

● Try to understand what this exercise tells you about your own desires.

After this really simple exercise, you should feel less weighed down by guilt about your jealousy and have a new perspective on your future, even if you don't have a completely concrete direction. Give yourself time: we're moving step by step.

Challenge
Live with your ideal rhythm

This week, you're going to change your rhythm. From today, you're going to break your usual routine. We all have habits and compulsions we have trouble giving up. From time to time, it's necessary to come up for air and see if that particular rhythm still suits you.

- Get up twenty minutes earlier or thirty minutes later than usual.
- If you usually have a shower before breakfast or after it, do the opposite!
- Leave home a little earlier or a little later.
- Change your mode of transport for getting to work. Why don't you try riding your bike or taking the bus?
- Have lunch a bit before your usual time. If you often eat a quick sandwich on the run, try a sit-down lunch. If you always take your time, try a quick snack.
- Modify the time you finish at work – resign yourself to working later if leaving early is unimaginable.
- If you usually hurry straight home after work, take your time, strolling for a bit – even if it's only for a quarter of an hour.
- Give your before-dinner drink a miss or, alternatively, try having that early evening glass you never usually allow yourself.
- Eat dinner at a different time.
- Go to bed at least an hour earlier or later, going with the flow.
- In short, change the times of your daily routines as much as possible, even if only by a few minutes.

Take stock: what did you like? Continue doing this for about a fortnight, to find a good rhythm. Stay open and experiment – it's the best way of knowing what suits you. And if your old way suited you better, return to it, but only after nine days, just to be sure that it's not just habit talking.

Magic
*Create
your ideal
surroundings*

Have you ever noticed how much better you feel when you're in an environment that suits you? This is why we often personalise our work desk with photos, or decorate our homes. But have you ever wondered what your ideal workplace would actually look like?

● Collect some interiors and travel magazines, or find a website with photographic inspiration.

● Take a few minutes to relax, making yourself comfortable and ensuring you won't be disturbed.

● Choose, without thinking about why, the photos that show a world you like.

● Find at least eighty photos.

● Choose the thirty you like the most and assemble them loosely into an inspiration board. Print it out if it's virtual.

● Take out your notebook and paste your images inside it.

● List what you notice about these images. Are there other people in the photos? Do the images represent a certain solitude? What are the colours like: rather soft, sombre, flashy ...? Is there space and sobriety or, on the contrary, a certain warmth and accumulation of objects?

● Be conscious of your ideal and of what it's possible to do to make your real space more like it.

● Make a list of the actions – small or large – you could take to make your surroundings more like your aspirations: replacing the curtains with wooden blinds; having a big clean-out and only keeping the essentials; buying a big poster of a beach scene; choosing a single colour and gradually replacing anything that doesn't match it, and so on.

● Immediately do three of the small things on your list that will transform your space.

● Plan your other actions: repainting the wall next month, or investing in a new, more compact computer before the end of the year. Make a date for each small and large step towards your ideal, but stay realistic: make sure you pay attention to your budgetary and time constraints.

Appreciate how nice it is to work in a space that matches your personality a little more.

Game

The law of five

Did you know that you come to resemble the five people you see the most often? If the majority of the people you see are negative, you'll have a tendency to be negative yourself. If you spend a large part of your time with aggressive people, this will have an effect on your capacity to stay zen. Let's look into this.

• Make a list of the people you see the most frequently. Not those that you love the most, nor those you'd prefer to spend your time with, but actually, mathematically, the people with whom you spend most of your days, evenings and weekends.

• Beside each of these people, note three characteristics about them that immediately come to mind. It doesn't matter if these make no sense, seem strange or not completely fair.

• Circle in red characteristics you'd prefer not to be around anymore and in green those you wish to experience more of.

• Is there more green or red? Is someone particularly red?

• Now list the qualities you'd like to develop and, beside each of these, try to find at least one person from your circle who possesses that quality.

• Gradually try to see the people who have the qualities you aspire to more often and gradually distance yourself from those who have too many of the characteristics that don't suit you.

• Who we spend time with says a lot about us. It can seem disloyal and futile to distance yourself from people you don't want to resemble, but in reality we need to try to understand why we see them. Often it's through obligation, habit and cowardice – so many feelings that weigh us down and that it's time to leave behind.

Challenge
Where are you at in life?

Part of getting to know yourself is also understanding where you're at in terms of satisfaction. Which areas of your life need stimulation? In which areas do you need help? Which plans should you implement the fastest? Let's take a closer look.

- Draw a big tree on a blank sheet of A4 paper, not drawing the branches for now, just the trunk.
- Each of the areas of your life will be represented by a branch. The happier you are in this area, the bigger and more beautiful and flourishing the branch will be.

The less satisfied you are, the smaller, barer and more broken the branch will be.

- Here is the list of areas: health, leisure, work, family, love life, friends, time for yourself.
- Label each branch with the area it represents.
- Look at your tree. It is balanced? Which branches are the most damaged? Which branches are in the best shape?

There are always some areas that are more thriving than others. Think about how you can lean on those in order to improve your tree as a whole. It can be frustrating to realise that several areas aren't what they should be, but it's essential to know where you're at so that you can consider how you might change things in your life.

Game
Relationship triangle quiz

Are you a victim, persecutor or rescuer? According to Steven Karpman, a psychiatrist who developed numerous theories of transactional analysis, the best known of which is his 'drama triangle', we experience relationships largely through roles. Which do you take on most often? Complete this quiz to find out.

1. Your partner wants to leave you.

[a] You shout at them and threaten them. It simply cannot happen this way!

[b] You think they might be depressed, and you ask how you can help them.

[c] You cry and convince yourself that it's all over.

[d] You try to understand and ask them how you can work it out together.

2. Your holiday is cancelled because you have to replace a sick colleague.

[a] You'll show that slacker what you're made of!

[b] You call them to suggest coming to see them and bringing them their medication.

[c] You knew those holidays were too good to be true.

[d] You do everything you can to postpone your holiday – getting refunds on your plane tickets, and so on.

3. Annie comes to visit you and tells you about her problems with her boss.

[a] You mock her a little and conclude that her boss was probably right after all.

[b] You find her boss's attitude so unacceptable that you suggest calling him or her.

[c] You reassure her by telling her how much harder it is for you.

[d] You listen to her with empathy and suggest two or three ideas for getting through it.

4. Your neighbour comes and yells at you because the rubbish bins are a mess.

[a] You yell louder. Seriously, who do they think they are?

[b] You go to the bins straightaway to sort the problem out.

[c] You break down and apologise to them between your sobs.

[d] You ask them if they'd like to have a drink and a chat, so that they can explain their concerns to you, because you haven't understood at all.

5. You're expecting your mother for dinner and she arrives twenty minutes early.

[a] You reproach her for being there already and turn it into a negative generalisation: 'You're incapable of respecting my privacy, and you've never been able to either.'

[b] You ask her if she's had a good day, if there is anything wrong, or if you can do something for her, because she really looks awful.

[c] You complain that it's just as well she's there because no one understands or respects you, and you've had enough of this cold-hearted world.

[d] You welcome her enthusiastically, offer her a drink and make her comfortable on the lounge while you finish a few things.

6. The grocer gets your change wrong.

[a] You turn it into a drama, calling them dishonest and any number of names.

[b] You point out to them that they're wrong, and that in fact they don't look too well, do they need a rest? You tell them you feel sorry for them.

[c] You don't say anything. Everyone's always ripping you off anyway, and you don't have the strength to stick up for yourself anymore.

[d] You let them know nicely and add that if it happens again you'll go to another grocer.

Results

Mostly [a]: the persecutor

You have a certain amount of aggression that needs to be expressed. You often take a combative position. You order other people around, and you find yourself humiliating or blaming them and thinking of them as inferior. If you detect this attitude in yourself, take a step back and try to deal with your nerves some other way, such as exercise or creativity.

Mostly [b]: the rescuer

You love to run to the aid of other people, and help them get out of difficult situations. The concern with this approach, though, is that our help is in reality often suffocating and ineffective. When you realise that you're about to adopt the position of rescuer, let it go and allow that person to deal with their own issue.

Mostly [c]: the victim

You attract other people by making them pity you. You put yourself into an inferior position out of fear of being jealous and you look for a persecutor to confirm to you that you're worthless. But you have more power than you think to get yourself out of sticky situations. When you catch yourself feeling sorry for yourself, analyse the situation. What's not right? What needs to be changed? What concrete actions can you take straightaway?

Mostly [d]

Well done! You stay out of Karpman's triangle with your great instincts. Keep up the good work.

Magic

*The stories
I tell*

Let's push the concept of creating positive scenarios a little farther.

- Make a list of what it frustrates you not to know: how your spouse feels, whether your boss is going to give you that raise, if your book is going to sell, if your children will be happy, if you're ever going to get married, and so on.
- Take the three things that make you the most anxious and, for each one, imagine an ideal scenario.
- Take plenty of time to write all the details of your story. For example, for whether your boss is going to give you a raise, imagine in your ideal scene that they compliment you. What do they say to you exactly? How do they congratulate you? How do they look? How exactly do they grant your raise to you? In what capacity?
- Savour your scenario and live it as if it were true. Portray it as realistically as possible, sensing the smells, the ambiance, the temperature, the sounds and sights.

After seventeen seconds, your brain will no longer know the difference between your scenario and reality. And so you should end up more relaxed and positive when you meet your boss to ask for the raise, since they've already given it to you, haven't they?

I'M RETURNING TO MY PAST

To see what your assets are more clearly –your most beautiful qualities, your ways of dealing with difficult situations – the best way is to go back over your history and understand how you've progressed, what your successes have been, what allowed them to come about; what your failures have been and what you learnt from them.

This is a week for nostalgia, for looking back one last time before moving forward with conviction towards your *ikigai*.

Let's think a little

When I was a visual arts student in Montreal, at Concordia University, I had some family issues that meant I was obliged to return to France. I decided to join my father in Nice, because I was already fascinated by the artists of the Nice school: Yves Klein, Ben, Sacha Sosno, César. I could really see myself as a student at Beaux-Arts de Nice, that superb school perched on a hill, a place of astonishing architecture with an ambiance all its own. So I did the entrance exam, very sure of myself because I'd just spent more than a year studying art in Montreal. During the exam, they asked me to draw a nude. Then there I was, in front of a panel of seven people who clearly saw no hint – not even the slightest – of talent in my drawing. I took out my portfolio: sketches in charcoal, watercolours, photos, sculptures. Nothing worked. 'If I were you, I'd think about another career', said the bitterest of them. 'Do a drawing course and come back in a few years', suggested the nicest. My self-esteem hit the ground. They were right. I was hopeless. Why bother?

Since this was the case, I decided to abandon everything. I was distraught. Goodbye, paintings and colours. Goodbye, art galleries, openings, admiration, life of my dreams. After having destroyed all my equipment and my work – three drawings, two sculptures and a page of a comic strip – I turned my back on fine art forever.

This was followed by desperate drifting: what could I do with my life now? I'll look for a menial job to keep myself busy over the summer and to fund possible future studies, but what? Close to depression, working in a horrible fast food joint for want of something better, without a future, without a project, I reached rock bottom.

It was a miracle that saved me and made some sense of this whole story. After months of burgers and fries and existential angst, I found, through a little ad, not a student job but a dream job: radio announcer. On one of my favourite stations. Every day I whispered scripts I'd written into the ears of thousands of people, talking about everything from opera to traffic jams on Nice's Promenade des Anglais, from cinema and jazz to the weather. The variety of subjects I wrote about and the pleasure I took in the words made me understand very quickly that writing was my life. That from now on, writing would be at the centre of everything I did. If I'd been accepted into the Beaux-Arts de Nice, I might never have discovered that I could write.

Failure = opportunity

Each failure is a chance to rebuild ourselves. To overhaul our lives and ask ourselves what's really important to us. Of course, it's hard to accept that a project we invested so much energy in will never come to fruition, but there's always a good reason or a great surprise hidden behind every failure if we just remain open.

Failing an end-of-year exam can mean that that subject is not the best path for us. Sure, it's annoying to have lost so many years, but it's always better than figuring that out ten years into your career. It could also be, on the contrary, confirmation that you're definitely on the right path and that there's no other. Suddenly, your failure beomes a chance to reignite your passion and to find solutions: sit the exam again the following year, making the most of it by going to study abroad, et cetera.

Professional failures can be more difficult to swallow. Being fired leads to an intensely stressful situation and creates significant financial problems. But it's still no less of a chance to ask yourself whether you might like to do something else. We're generally lucky in the Western world to have a safety net. With unemployment benefits that allow us to keep going and government funding for study and housing assistance, it's possible to imagine taking risks, and making the most of a failure by trying something else.

Create luck by bouncing back

There's no such thing as good fortune, or a lucky star. It's not what happens to you that counts, but what you do with it. Luck is simply strength: it's an attitude you take towards the unpredictability of life. Some people will see being fired as the end of the world, struggling against a closed door, falling into a downward spiral of disgust, throwing in the towel. Others will say to themselves: 'How lucky am I? I'm finally going to have some time to myself. I'll be able to go back and do some study. I'll be able to change my life.' Serious blow or marvellous opportunity – it's up to you to decide.

When one door closes, another really does always open. Anything is possible. You can reinvent yourself. It's not about denying the past and starting from scratch. Besides, the expression 'starting from scratch' makes no sense, since we've always accumulated experience, skills, know-how and ideas along the way. We never start completely from scratch, even when we radically change our field of study or work. Our past experience, even if it has nothing to do with what we're starting, allows us to look at our field of interest with fresh eyes. Stop seeing the detours in your career as negatives, and instead try to see what useful things you can bring from them to your new path.

Rest on your
past successes

What have you succeeded in? What are your greatest achievements? These successful attempts show you that it's possible to get there. If you've already been able to achieve things that once seemed impossible to you, then you can do it again.

You think you've never succeeded in anything? Take the example of walking. When you were a baby, you tried to walk and you failed, falling dozens of times, until the day when you took your first step. That's a success. In the same way, you learnt to read and write, to dance and perhaps to drive. And I'm sure all of that seemed impossible to you at the beginning, discouraging, unachievable. It's good to remind yourself of your successes – they'll help you get through your life's difficult moments.

Detect your
true motivation

Look at your life's journey and think about what spurs you to action. Think about the biggest challenges that you've taken on and look at how you succeeded. What were your strengths? What qualities did you put to work to reach your goals? What created problems for you? And, above all, what motivated you? What was it that allowed you to hold on through difficulties? What was it that allowed you to believe you'd be able to meet the challenge?

Knowing your own history well – its uncertainties, its failures, its successes – and thinking through it, will allow you to work out what you can count on in the future. Your greatest successes will educate you about the way you work – something we'll explore further with several games in the second part of this chapter.

Kintsugi, valuing life's accidents

In Japan, they really prize old objects that have seen some life. The majority of people distinctly prefer an old cast-iron teapot marked by time to a completely shiny, new teapot. It's cultural. This veneration of the well-worn patina of time goes even further with the art of *kintsugi*. It's about repairing broken porcelain with gold.

This art form, which appeared at the end the 15th century, was begun by Japanese artists who were seeking an aesthetically pleasing way of repairing china. And so, rather than hiding the repairs, which is often impossible or not aesthetically pleasing, they decided to make a feature of them. Thus breaking a pot no longer meant throwing it away: quite the contrary. The holes and cracks were filled with golden lacquer. In this way, old objects that have been broken and repaired take on even greater value. Literally.

Used objects that become ever more precious – it's a beautiful idea that goes against the flow of Western society, enamoured as we are with the new, and with constantly replacing objects that still function. Don't be afraid to show off your wounds, your failures and your past, however dark – be proud of them. Visualise yourself as having been repaired *kintsugi*-style and be aware that this is what makes you unique, precious and irreplaceable.

Let's play a little

Now that you've become aware of your own history, let's dig a little deeper into the subject and linger a little over what has made you the unique being you are today: What are your assets? Your driving forces? Your strengths? Your weaknesses? Let's have a look at what your past has brought you in order to gain a better idea of what to do with it next.

Magic
Body memory

Since you've already achieved success, you know that it's possible. This brief visualisation will allow you to embed in your body that feeling of confidence that comes from your past successes and to call on it again as often as you need to with a simple gesture.

- Make yourself comfortable in a place where you won't be disturbed. Read the following visualisation aloud, recording it on your smartphone, or ask someone you trust to read it to you.
- Take three deep breaths and start listening.

You're in a beautiful garden, a place that suits you and where you feel good. You're one year old. You start to try to walk. You hold on to the garden wall, you fall down, you get up again, then you start again until you take your first step. You're very proud. Take the time to savour this feeling of victory. What's happening within your body? Which muscles are engaged? Which are relaxed? What's your heartbeat like? How's your breathing? Hold onto this feeling and make a simple gesture that you can reproduce easily. This gesture will record this sensation of wellbeing in your body. Now think about another, more recent victory. See yourself in the process of succeeding. Put yourself back in that moment and observe your feelings in the same way. Are they the same? What's different about them? Make your chosen gesture again and ask your body to record this feeling of confidence, wellbeing and satisfaction. Take three deep breaths and return to the present at your own pace.

With this anchoring exercise, you've created a magic button for wellbeing and confidence. You can reactivate this feeling whenever you feel the need.

Game

Discover the gifts hidden in your failures

Have you failed many times? So much the better! Let's have a little look at what these failures have given you; let's search for the gifts hidden in adversity.

● Take your notebook and write down your three most memorable/painful failures. For each of these failures find at least two advantages you were able to draw from them.

● For example, you failed the entrance exam for medical school, but that allowed you to discover naturopathy and train in this discipline, which allowed you to complete your studies a little faster and to start earning your living earlier in a field that suits you better.

● If you can't find the benefits of a particular failure, it's perhaps still too fresh and too raw. Don't hesitate to ask a kind person from your circle for help – they'll definitely have some interesting suggestions for you.

● Close your notebook, sincerely thank life for bringing you through these ordeals, and recognise that you wouldn't be where you are today without them. Feel real gratitude.

It's good to know that whatever you attempt, life will be there to support you and to offer you a way out if you make a mistake. Yes, you do have the right to make mistakes. Good news, right?

Challenge

Long live failure!

Today is the festival of failure. We're really going to have fun – oh yes we will, you'll see. Your aim for today: to fail … It's not as easy as it seems.

● Start off by listing about twenty things in your notebook that you don't do for fear of failing. For example: asking for a raise, going surfing for the first time, beginning to write a book, doing a cooking course …

● Make a second list of the little things you don't know how to do, the ones you've already tried that clearly aren't your thing, which annoy you: making béchamel sauce, drawing a cat, winning at Monopoly …

Choose five things from your two lists that you can try or retry this very day.

● With each of the things you've decided to try, do your best and ask for help and advice from the people in your circle.

● With some you'll succeed, of course. And if you succeed at all of them, you must keep on trying new experiences until you fail at least once.

● In the evening, take up your notebook and record your feelings and experiences: what things did you fail at? Did you succeed with more things than you thought you would? What effect did that have on you?

Trying things you thought you couldn't succeed at and managing to do them is the best ego boost there is.

Game
The timeline of your life

To really become conscious of your own history and the impact it's had on you, we're going to create a timeline of your successes and failures.

- Take your notebook and list ten of your most important successes in the order they come to you, without censorship or judgement, taking whatever comes: Passing your final year of high school? Going out with the cutest guy in fifth grade? Becoming marketing director at the age of twenty-two? Being exhibited in a prestigious gallery? Freeing yourself from emotional dependence?
- Then make a list of your failures, your bitter regrets, your defeats. In the same way, record whatever comes without prioritising by importance or value. Again, list ten.
- Draw a timeline and place on it each of the events you've recorded.
- Put the events that eventually turned out to be positive above the line and the ones that turned out negative below the line.

For example, going out with the cutest guy is at first glance positive, but if he turned out to be an idiot then you may put it under the line. Failing your final-year exams is negative, but if that allowed to you take a step back and take the time to think about what you wanted to study next, you put it above the line.

- Examine your timeline and compare your positive and negative events. Also note that you've come through numerous difficult situations brilliantly and accomplished lots of things you can be proud of.

Magic
Discover your assets

Discover your most solid assets so that you know what you can rely on in difficult moments.

- Take your notebook and list your three greatest accomplishments, the ones you're proudest of.
- Consider each success and think about what allowed you to get there: Were you reckless? Persistent? Idealistic? Did you work day and night? Did you know how to make the right decision at the right moment?
- If you think you were just lucky or it was an accident that allowed you to succeed, try to dig a little deeper and ask yourself which of

your qualities your success would not have been possible without.

● Find at least three assets for each of your successes.

Are there some that recur several times? These are your most important assets.

● For each of these assets, turn to a fresh page of your notebook and write sentences including them that start with 'I': 'I'm tenacious', 'I'm capable of working as hard as necessary to reach my goals', 'I make good decisions'.

● To really internalise these sentences, read them aloud, either addressing someone else or, if you can't face that, addressing yourself in the mirror.

After a failure or in a moment of doubt, you can return to your notebook to find this list of irrefutable assets – because they've supported you in the past, they will at least be enough to give you a boost, or even some ideas for getting through a bad patch.

Challenge
A new experience every hour

Warning: this is going to be a very full day, so it's better to complete this challenge on a day off or, if that's not possible, spread it throughout the week. The idea is to have seven new experiences in a single day.

● Find fifteen ideas of things you've never done and that you could try today: eating oysters, going for a promotion, reading a magazine in another language, watching the first episode of a series you don't know, going to the movies alone, drinking a guava juice, and so on.

● Choose the seven that tempt you most and create a timetable for your day (or week, for those who have to space this challenge out): 10 am, try a cronut, 11 am, read something by that popular new author, 12 pm have lunch alone outside, and so on.

● As your day progresses, make notes in your notebook about your feelings and reactions: Is the new thing you're trying nice? Funny? Stressful?

Confronting novelty is the best way to evolve. We're made for discovery, and introducing some novelty into your life will give your projects extra momentum. If you'd like to, you can try to follow this challenge throughout the year by attempting a new thing each week.

Magic

I'm so lucky

Luck, as we've already seen, is above all a question of how you react to what life throws at you. Let's look back at your strokes of luck and discover the role you have played in your good fortune.

● Take your notebook and make a list of every time you were lucky. Write whatever comes, without taking the time to think, and try to find at least ten. They could be major or really small: the day you passed that exam without having revised enough, the day you found a large banknote at the pool, that apartment you snapped up that was well below market price ...

● Circle the things on your list that have made the biggest mark on you, choosing at least three.

● For each of these 'strokes of luck' find three things you did that allowed this event to happen. For example, with the banknote at the pool: you were observant, you reacted, you quickly made a decision that made you the new owner of the note.

● If you really can't see that you played any role, persist and look harder, because this one's probably even more important – it's hiding a talent so deeply embedded in you that you don't even see it in yourself anymore.

● Take the example of the apartment below market price: you were tenacious (you put in hours of research) or you were sociable (you re-established contact with a friend who's become an estate agent), you were quick (you visited and submitted your forms straightaway, and were the first to respond to the advertisement), you dared to ask (a favour from a friend, help from your family, and so on).

● Examine all the things you did in order to bring about your luck. These are the attitudes you can reproduce from now on to be lucky more often.

Now you know that although you're lucky, your good fortune didn't just fall from the sky. That can be hard to hear, but the good news is that in fact, everything is in your own hands and from today you have the know-how to create luck for yourself!

Books for bouncing back

For understanding resilience:
Resilience: How Your Inner Strength Can Set You Free from the Past, Boris Cyrulnik, Jeremy P. Tarcher, 2009

For seeing the good in something when it all seems bad:
Learned Optimism: How to Change Your Mind and Your Life, Martin E.P. Seligman, Pocket Books, 1998

For no longer allowing your past to weigh you down:
Recovering from Childhood Wounds, Jacques Lecomte, Free Association Press, 2006

For finding out what you really want to do:
Louder Than Words: Harness the Power of Your Authentic Voice, Todd Henry, Penguin, 2015

I'M ADOPTING SELF-COMPASSION

Here you are with a better idea of who you are, and a clearer picture of your strengths and your weaknesses. When we bring our pluses and minuses to light, we do it so we can accept them completely. That's the work we're going to do this week.

You cannot know yourself without accepting yourself, as you will always try to hide from yourself the parts you don't accept.

Learning to love yourself fully is your mission this week. Yes, yes, you'll see, it's very doable!

Let's think a little

was always slightly ashamed of who I was. As a child, it was because I didn't like the same things as the other kids – I liked black-and-white films much more than Japanese animé, for example. As a teen, it was because I had very wide musical tastes – from Bob Marley to Nirvana via the 1980s French pop of Étienne Daho – and this was the time of life when I should have been choosing one tribe or the other, or at least that's what I thought. And so I'd always adopted the habit of hiding my preferences, of pretending to like what everyone else was crazy about so that people would also like me. I did this to the point where I ended up no longer knowing what really gave me pleasure.

I'd also never been very proud of myself: my clumsiness, my inability to be popular at school. I concentrated a lot on what I didn't know how to do, on what I had no talent for, scolding myself over and over again all day long. This didn't get any better once I was an adult: 'Pfft! What an idiot! I didn't even have the guts to say hello; they'll think I'm a snob', 'What a nitwit, I've laddered my stockings again!', 'I couldn't do it anyway, I'm too shy', and so on.

I believe you could say that I hated myself. I was my own worst enemy. I was always shooting myself in the foot. And this is how I came to be interested in personal development. At first I read lots of books, then I undertook some therapy with a sophrologist. I made such leaps and bounds with sophrology that I wanted to try other therapies: I sorted out my fears with hypnosis, I discovered body memory with an energetic healer who made me understand so many things despite hardly saying anything! I also tried gestalt therapy and family constellations. When four different therapists told me the same thing: 'Be kind to yourself', I didn't understand what they meant. Since they were all in agreement without conferring, I bought a book on the subject anyway: *The Mindful Path to Self-compassion: Freeing Yourself from Destructive Thoughts and Emotions* by Christopher K. Germer (Guilford Press). This book was a turning point. My nasty little inner voice wasn't the coach I'd imagined it to be, but an obstacle to my happiness. The self-reproaches I'd practised for so long didn't help me to progress, but held me back even more. This book explained how essential it is to be good to yourself in order to be the same to other people. It was a real shock, because I realised that on top of being really hard on myself, I was extremely demanding and rigid with other people. Its advice and short meditations allowed me to evolve. Above all, I realised that not only did I have the right to be gentle with myself, but on top of that, doing so would have beneficial effects on everyone around me. And so I was permanently set on the path towards self-compassion.

To give yourself permission to wish for good things and forbid yourself from being unkind to yourself is to open up to a lighter and more peaceful life, and to free up energy to move forward rather than complain. It's a real liberation.

How your inner tyrant spoils your life

When you break a glass you love, what's your reaction? 'I'm hopeless, I'm such an idiot, I can't take being so clumsy anymore!' Something like that? And you find that completely normal. Yet imagine you have invited round a guest, a friend you really treasure. She asks for a glass of water. You give it to her in the glass you love so much, and it slips out of her hands and breaks into a thousand pieces. After a second of annoyance, you'll say to your terribly embarrassed friend who's apologising profusely: 'Oh, it's nothing, don't worry about it!' Even if you're a little bit annoyed with her, even if her clumsiness gets on your nerves, you'd never say to her what you said to yourself. It wouldn't even occur to you to treat her like that. And yet, you find it normal to insult and reproach yourself repeatedly in the same situation. Can you see the problem?

How we hurt ourselves daily

Every single day we insult ourselves, kicking ourselves in the backside and demonstrating zero tolerance of our weaknesses. Even the same ones that we accept very easily – and actually find endearing – in other people.

Try to notice in your everyday life how many times per day you insult yourself or make disparaging remarks – it's enlightening! Some people would argue that being hard on yourself allows for progress and self-improvement. That was my own credo for a long time, but I no longer believe it. You burn yourself out by being mean, while on the other hand, when you tolerate even your worst weaknesses, you end up gaining the greatest returns. If we go back to the example of the glass: criticising myself and crying over it won't help me make progress. I'll still break another glass, a cup, a teapot and a heap of other objects in my life. In contrast, if I'm gentle with myself, and understand that that's the way it is and I can't change anything about it now, I can buy myself the gift of a lovely new glass to replace it and make a deal with myself not to be so upset every time I break something. I can also try other solutions: buy a less fragile glass, or one in resin that doesn't break. By being kind to myself, I find solutions that make my life easier.

My gentleness leads me to accept who I am: yes, I definitely do break glasses, but I'm a pro at finding other beautiful ones and at hunting them out in second-hand shops, so it's not a problem! Accepting myself allows me to be creative, reinforcing my personality and what makes me a unique being.

Why it's necessary to be kind to yourself

Being mean to yourself doesn't do you any good. On the contrary, when we manage to accept ourselves, to tolerate our darker side, to believe in ourselves despite our bad points, we can move forward and more easily create a life that suits us.

The example of the glass is simplistic, but it allows us to understand the mechanism. Let's see how it works on a professional level. One of my clients who completed my course in life coaching and energy therapy asked me, when she was launching her own practice: 'Which of my specialties should I highlight? Coaching is serious and professional, energy therapy a little more mystical and strange, but very effective. I don't know what to do – I'm afraid that one will discredit the other.' She was ready to obliterate and hide half of her knowledge just to please an imaginary clientele who wouldn't have appreciated one or the other of her facets. I answered that she should mix the two. Then, one day, she decided to offer a course on energetic coaching and very quickly experienced enormous success. Magic? No, just logic: the closer you are to your true self, the more you accept every facet of your personality, the more special you will be and thus the more irreplaceable!

Reiki, the art of self-healing

Reiki is a Japanese healing method of laying on hands. During their training, the therapist is initiated by a master who connects them to the universal source and teaches them the rituals for healing as well as the rules for the way of life. The *reiki* therapist must apply the following five rules for life:

- Do not become angry.
- Worry about nothing.
- Express your gratitude.
- Be diligent in your work.
- Be kind to others and to yourself.

The first person the therapist is led to care for is themselves. They learn the ritual of self-healing and must repeat it regularly in order to continue practising. It's a process that takes about thirty minutes, during which you apply your hands to precise zones on your body, from toes to head, keeping to a minute for each point. It's this self-healing that allows the therapist to heal others. This ritual is taught to first-level students who, even if they don't necessarily continue their training, can learn *reiki* just to heal themselves.

Let's play a little

You can teach yourself self-compassion, and the best way to do that is through play. So this week, even more than the others, let's have fun! Are you capable of being kind to yourself for an entire day? Let's find out.

Challenge
Marathon of gentleness

Your first challenge this week is to be kind to yourself for twenty-four hours. This may seem easy, but be warned: you must respect the rules of the game, which are listed below.

- No insulting yourself, even in your head.
- No mean nicknames: not even the ones that pretend to be kind like 'silly nana' or 'goose'.
- You can be mean to others to compensate, but it's very unlikely that you'll want to.
- If you catch yourself starting a sentence of unkind internal self-talk, stop it straightaway and turn it around to say something nice to yourself instead.
- For example, if you've forgotten a meeting, don't say to yourself: 'God, I'm stupid!', but instead say: 'I clearly don't want to go that much, so maybe it's for the best.'
- If you don't manage to stop yourself and you end up saying something mean to yourself, treat yourself as you would a friend: excuse yourself and say that you weren't really thinking about what you were saying.
- Make notes in your notebook throughout this process about how you're feeling, what you stopped yourself from saying and what you replaced it with.
- At the end of the twenty-four hours, take stock. How do you feel? What was the hardest thing to do? Which situations posed the biggest problem for you?

If you felt that this challenge did you good, ask yourself if it's appropriate to continue being unkind to yourself in the old way. Could you continue?

Challenge
Twenty-one days of gentleness

They say that something we can keep up for twenty-one days becomes a habit for life. If you were convinced by your twenty-four hours of gentleness, take it up a notch with this challenge. The rules remain the same, with a couple of important additions.

● Get hold of an elastic band or elastic bracelet that's easy to remove and is waterproof, which you'll wear 24/7 for the entire duration of the challenge.

● Each time you catch yourself insulting yourself or reproaching yourself for something, change which arm the bracelet is on, and return your day-count to zero.

● Yes, even if you've managed eighteen days, you must start again at day one.

● Yes, you may count the previous challenge from yesterday as day one of this challenge.

After twenty-one days of honing your cruelty-free approach, take stock of your joie de vivre and wellbeing: how do you feel?

Magic
Caring visualisation

The most direct way to show yourself compassion is this restorative visualisation.

● Make yourself comfortable in a place where you can be sure you won't be disturbed.

● Record the text below beforehand, reading in a clear voice, or ask someone else to read it to you.

Close your eyes and feel all the weight of your body pushing down into the chair or mat. Breathe deeply so that you can feel your belly expand as you inhale and fall as you exhale. Repeat this deep breathing ten more times. Visualise a path. Walk forwards slowly, then come to a place that appeals to you, a little haven of peace where you'd like to settle yourself down. Sense how lovely it smells, enjoy the light breeze that brushes against your cheek, taste the drink you feel like drinking, curl up in the chair that looks the cosiest and softest. Once you're comfortably settled, imagine you have a newborn in your arms, a tiny being who needs infinite love. Cuddle it, give it the unconditional love that all babies deserve. Cradle and rock it, enjoy how good it feels in your arms, how you're fulfilling its need for love and affection. This baby is you. You deserve to be loved unconditionally. You were also once a newborn, and today you still have the human right to unconditional love. Continue to caress and cradle the baby of your conscious mind, bearing in mind that this child really is you. The more you rock it, the more luminous it becomes, until it's nothing but a beautiful light that enters your heart and radiates through your whole body. Feel the warmth of this light of pure love as it pervades your entire being. Feel how good it is to be loved. Make a deal with yourself that you'll always give yourself love of this quality. Glowing and relaxed, little by little, return to the present by concentrating on your breath, then by gradually moving your hands and feet and, finally, by opening your eyes, all at your own pace.

This visualisation will allow you to realise how much you're justified in giving yourself the love you need so much. Using this image of the fragile newborn you must care for, you should gradually move towards showing yourself greater kindness. Record your progress in your notebook; it could be interesting to return to in a few months, to give you a sense of how far you've come.

Game

List your points of pride

Establishing this ritual will make you realise how many amazing things you do each day.

● Each day, at the end of the day, note three things that happened that you're proud of.

● At the table, make use of the mealtime to talk about them: each person can say the three things they're proud of that day. Sharing them makes them even greater.

● If you live alone, you can post them on social media or even arrange a daily phone call with someone who's on the same path as you.

● Whether they're really small – I made a fantastic cheese sauce, I went shopping without buying anything useless – or really big – I passed an exam, I finally talked to my parents about a worry that's been weighing on me – the important thing is to find three.

● Listening to other people's reasons for pride will inspire you, and the idea of giving three each day will encourage you to have more reasons to be proud.

We congratulate ourselves too rarely for our great successes and almost never for our small victories. Even if you only manage to maintain this ritual for a few weeks, you should feel a clear lift in your self-confidence.

Challenge

The diary of pleasures

Why limit your diary to mandatory meetings and other obligations? Let's add a few pleasures to vary it a little.

● In your notebook, list the things that give you pleasure, the really simple, free or inexpensive things, those that do you good and are easily accessible.

● Try to find at least twenty-five of them. This could range from a little cup of piping-hot tea in the morning to watching the sunset, flicking through an interiors magazine or going for a walk in nature, or even just letting a square of dark chocolate melt in your mouth.

- Don't hold back – just write down whatever comes, even if you suddenly realise it's too complicated or too expensive. There'll always be time to refine your list.
- Once you have twenty-five ideas, cross out the five that seem the least appealing and circle the five that excite you the most.
- Then take your diary and add one of your twenty ideas to each day of the coming month. Feel free to repeat the five pleasures you've circled.

From now on, be meticulous about timetabling your pleasures. And of course, nothing is stopping you from adding some more spontaneously! See how much giving yourself dates with pleasure reconciles you to the obligations in your diary!

Magic
Changing your inner coach

If your inner voice is often mean, are you recluctant to tone it down for fear of making yourself soft? What if you just transformed it into your inner coach?

- Remind yourself of the unkind sentences you often repeat to yourself.
- If you can't think of them now, make a note of them over the next few days as they come up.
- Take your three most commonly repeated sentences and, for each one, try to hear the inner voice that repeats them. Is the voice female or male? Is it someone you know? Or is it someone who corresponds to an archetype (old school teacher, witch, bearded guru …)?
- Once you've identified a real or imaginary person saying these unpleasant things over and over inside your head, visualise them standing in front of you. Thank them for the help they've given you to this point and say to them that today they're no longer relevant, that you've evolved and you no longer need them. Make them realise that they need to leave straightaway.
- So as not to leave the job vacant and tempt that person to return, choose your new inner coach. This could be a real or imaginary person, a celebrity or film character, but preferably someone you don't know and that you're unlikely ever to meet in real life.
- Short of ideas? It could be someone who makes you smile;

not necessarily someone funny, just someone who it pleases you to imagine coaching you. Just like in the other exercises, don't over-think it, but approach it spontaneously. Don't hold back. Even if you think of Britney Spears, try not to find someone else because she seems a stupid choice to you. On the contrary, the more ridiculous you find it, the more good it will do you!

● Some examples: Wonder Woman, Jerry Seinfeld, Aretha Franklin, Oprah, Jean-Paul Sartre, Tina Fey, Bugs Bunny, Beyoncé …

● Brief your coach: their role is to neutralise the mean little phrases, to reframe and reformulate each instance of 'I'm hopeless' into 'You won't always do everything perfectly because you're a human being, not a robot.'

The act of replacing the mean little voice in your head with a voice that's sympathetic will transform your interior conversation while also boosting your morale. Why didn't you think of this before?!

Game

My shadows

To accept and own your darker side is to ensure ongoing self-respect. Here's a little game to get you on your way.

● Make a note in your notebook of the things you like least about yourself. These could be physical, psychological, intellectual …

● Find at least ten big concerns.

● Choose the three worst ones, from your perspective.

● Stand in front of a mirror and, for each one, say the sentence 'I am [insert your worry] and I love and accept myself' five times, taking time over each of your words.

Then you can end by saying, 'I accept myself fully.'

The act of saying that you accept yourself despite your darkest sides is extremely powerful. Repeat this little game from time to time and watch how your way of seeing yourself is turned on its head.

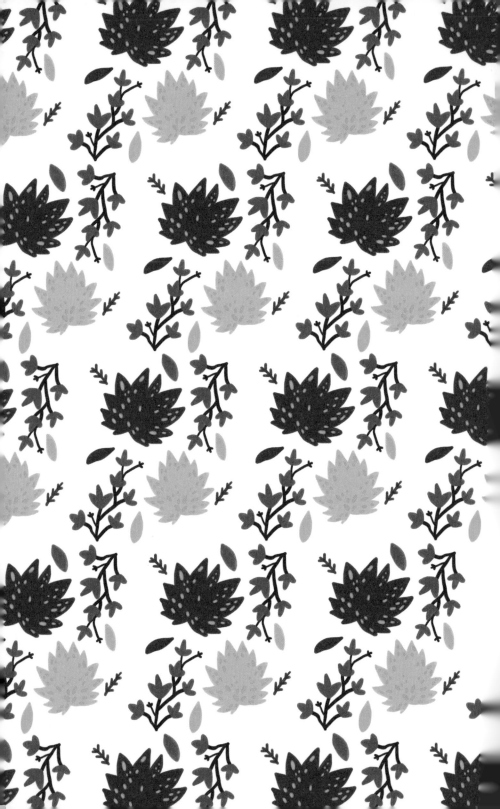

I'M FINDING
MY MISSION

After the long process of clearing your path, **here you are, finally ready to discover your mission in life** – which is really just a fancy way of saying what you could, would like to, and should transmit to the world.

Off we go, for a week full of discoveries.

Let's think a little

For a long time, I found it very difficult to introduce myself to other people when networking or at parties full of strangers. It was something that made me nervous to the point where I went as little as possible to evenings out where I wouldn't know anyone. Already, as an introvert, I had trouble making the effort to form new acquaintances, but not having an exact profession really made my life complicated at these get-togethers.

What do you say when you do dozens of different things? How do you answer the question 'So what do you do?' when you only do temporary things or lots of things at once? Or a single thing, but one you know will only be fleeting? It's hard to hold people's interest with a long list of 'I do this and that and this and that'. It's complicated, being taken seriously, when you say: 'At the moment I'm training in naturopathy, I'm giving courses on luck, I'm preparing an exhibition of my Polaroids and I'm writing a book on happiness.' Too many different fields loses the listener and starts to look suspicious. This is even more the case, given I have a tendency to work in professions with a reputation for being poorly paid. That inevitably triggers the irritating question: 'Okay, but what do you do to earn a living?', which leads to the answer that exasperates everyone: 'Well, all of the above', which brings the conversation to a dangerous precipice of mixed incomprehension, envy and suspicion. This generally results in either an unpleasant feeling of inferiority for the other person, who suddenly feels called into question, no longer able to justify their creative inertia with 'Oh, but that doesn't pay anyway'. Or even worse, to a conclusion that, although unspoken, can be strongly felt: 'Pfft, not another wannabe.' The result: in both cases, I come across to strangers as terribly unpleasant and I quickly put them off.

Sometimes, I tried to keep it minimal: 'At the moment, I'm studying hypnosis', but then people still asked all the same questions and really dug into that one subject, which I didn't find fascinating enough to talk about for the whole evening. It locked me into a role that wasn't mine, closing the door on the possibility of jumping into the conversation when someone else mentioned their love of Polaroids, and making me bite my tongue so as not to butt in when someone said that these days you can't earn a living as an author. Nothing about this approach made the evening any more pleasant for me.

It was a lecture by filmmaker and motivational speaker Adam Leipzig that saved my networking life: 'How to know your life purpose in five minutes'. He explained that being asked the question 'What do you do for a living?' and answering with a profession – engineer, doctor, and so on – isn't interesting and doesn't allow the person you're meeting to be curious. He advised answering instead with your mission in life. Ha, ha! Great advice! But I still have to work out what my mission is! And how to summarise it. At that point, he gave us a method of astonishing simplicity: it's what you do best (or for people who are good at lots of things, the one thing you're clearly best at), who you do it for, and why you do it. Which gives us, for example: 'I fix computer systems for stock traders, because I love that stimulating environment and I always find quick solutions.' Much more interesting than: 'I'm a network engineer.' And you can jump in: 'Ah! And what is it about the stock exchange that you find stimulating?' Another example: 'I write books for the general public in the area of wellbeing, because I love learning new things and making them accessible.' Much more open than: 'I write self-help books.' With this kind of approach, opening up the conversation becomes easier too. The response could even be more open: 'I practise different artforms for all types of audiences, because I love to express what I feel and to rally people to subjects that move me.' It says a lot more than: 'I'm a photographer, painter, writer and sculptor.' This really simple discovery transformed my evenings out, because suddenly people introduced themselves in the same way and everything became much more interesting.

The importance of bringing meaning to what we do

That little exercise in introductions has the advantage of teaching us the importance of knowing why, and for whom, we do things. It's this meaning that makes life interesting for us, as well as for the people with whom we talk about it.

Even when it comes to the smallest everyday things, we feel more connected to, and happier with our lives, if we know why we do them. Let's take a very simple example that affects the large majority of us: taking out the bins. It's no one's passion, but who likes living with the smell of old rubbish? We take the rubbish out because we make the choice to live in a clean and healthy environment. Reminding ourselves of that makes the chore lighter.

In every profession, some aspects are less interesting than others, and even the fields that people dream about have their difficult aspects. If you're a model, you have to maintain your body, do lots of exercise, eat light and healthy food. If you're a photographer, there are lots of things to do that aren't artistic at all: sorting and cleaning equipment, chasing clients for payment, seeking out new clients, feeding social networks with images to attract more people. If you're a baker, you must get up at dawn, work standing up, and even work on weekends. If you're a copywriter or graphic designer, you have to attend endless meetings where no one can ever agree, work crazy hours when deadlines are looming and set aside your creative ideas to satisfy your clients' wishes. In the same way, if you know the reason why you do these things, they'll seem much more manageable.

The different types of life mission

We can't all change the world in the same way, but each of us has gifts, qualities and skills that allow us to move forward in our own direction. At the start, this journey can feel frightening, and it's difficult to begin when you feel intimidated and discouraged. If you can see where to go but you don't want to go there – if something is holding you back – it's probably because you're on the right track!

To narrow down your life mission, you can ask yourself what you do naturally already that brings good to the world. For example, do you love explaining things, and do people sometimes call you 'Mr/Mrs/Ms Know-it-all'? Your mission is surely in the area of teaching and passing on your knowledge. Are you always helping others, carrying shopping for your elderly neighbour, helping the visually impaired to cross the road? Your mission will be in the area of serving or caring for others. If you're always making practical objects and transforming objects to make them more useful, inventing solutions and suggesting new ways of doing things to those around you, your life mission will be in innovation and research. These are very large fields that can be explored in many different ways, but they give you a general idea.

Viktor Frankl and logotherapy

During his internment in concentration camps, the psychiatrist Viktor Frankl noticed that the people who held up best, fell ill less often, and didn't give in to despair were, contrary to what you might think, not those who were in the best physical shape, but rather those who had a long-term goal. 'When I get out of here, I'm going to publish a book', 'I have to hold on for my daughter who's still in

Paris', and so on. What the goal was didn't matter, it was the fact of having one that seemed to make the suffering easier to bear and keep illness at bay.

After he was liberated from the camps, he created logotherapy, a technique based on discovering the meaning of your own life, because according to him, it is only this meaning that can allow us to be happy or at least get rid of neuroses. The therapist doesn't show the patient the way, but helps them to find their values, motivations and true desires themselves.

Gratitude for finding meaning

Reconnecting with gratitude can be a great source of meaning. Why and for whom do you do what you do each day? Don't try to answer these questions, which can sometimes be complex, but allow the ideas to come by making a list of the things you'd like to thank life for. These could be really little things, like: the chance to learn how to swim and to have access to a pool from time to time, the possibility of getting a massage once every three months ... or really big, like: the possibility of having children, the joy of having a boyfriend/girlfriend, being able to experience being elected as your local MP ... Make your list without limiting yourself: you'll see that a general pattern will appear. Maybe lots of the items on this list will be centred around one or two main subjects – if so, this is where you should look for your meaning.

Books that will provide meaning

For finding a direction:
Find Your Why, Simon Sinek, Penguin, 2018

For finding your place in the world:
The Fear of Insignificance, Carlo Strenger, Palgrave Macmillan, 2011

Man's Search for Meaning, Victor Frankl, Beacon Press, 2008 (originally published 1946)

For finding the middle path:
An Appeal to the World: The Way to Peace in a Time of Division, Dalai Lama, William Morrow, 2017

For finding happiness in meaning:
Flourish, Martin E.P. Seligman, Free Press, 2011

Kyudo, archery as self-mastery

This form of archery practice consists of finding the perfect movement to transcend both the mind and the body at the same time. The gestures are stylised and very symbolic, the aim being to pierce a sheet of paper by straining your muscles as little as possible. The archer must take into account both the context and the other people present to aim as surely as possible.

To progress in 'the way of the bow', the archer must prove their sincerity and perseverance, and make advances in their inner search. They must learn to let go and abandon their ego to reconnect with their deepest self. It's this deep inner self that makes it possible to perform the correct moves. The true target to attain is the internal one rather than the paper one in the distance.

In the same way, to find your mission in life and aim squarely at your own path, you must let go of appearances, detach yourself from the wishes of other people and from false beliefs, and discover who you really are when artifice falls away.

Let's play a little

Enough of cleaning house. Here you are, finally ready to fill your space with true intentions that are yours alone. This week, we're going to explore your imagination and try to create your ideal life.

Game

Excavating your true desires

Today is your funeral. No, don't be sad – it's a little game for bringing to the surface what really matters to you.

● Take out your notebook and a pen to record what comes to you immediately after this little visualisation.

● Record the text below so you can listen to it afterwards, or ask someone you trust to read it to you.

● Make yourself comfortable and make sure you won't be disturbed for at least twenty minutes.

Close your eyes and concentrate on your breathing, counting ten deep breaths, then blow out hard, as far as you can, letting go of everything that's on your mind. There's a path in front of you: make your way up it slowly. A little further on, on the right, there's a gathering. Everyone is in black and people are sad. All your nearest and dearest are there, your family and friends. You approach, but no one sees you. There's a coffin in the middle: it's yours. Get into it and watch the people pass by, listening to what they say. Remember every little detail, the speeches, which of your qualities they highlight, what they say about your career and about what you did for others. What do they thank you for? In what way will you be a loss to humanity? Listen carefully to everything that's said. Concentrate again on your breathing and open your eyes.

● Make a note straightaway of what struck you, what people said about you, what you heard.

Imagining yourself dead brings out all the desires and ideas that we don't let ourselves think about – having them come out of other people's mouths makes them seem acceptable. Even if what comes out seems outlandish or annoying, take it into account. These ideas offer precious information on the thoughts you hide, even from yourself.

Magic
Creating the
collage of
your future

Create a mood board for your ideal life.
● Take a pile of old magazines. Ideally, they'll have different themes: travel, interiors, fashion, cooking, and so on.
● Gather together an A3 sheet of cardboard, scissors and glue.
● The more magazines there are, the better. Take the time to collect them from your friends, family and neighbours – everyone always has lots of magazines lying around the house you will be able to use.
● Don't succumb to the temptation of doing this exercise digitally with images found on the internet, because you'll lose a lot of the spontaneity.
● Flick through the magazines and, as soon as you happen upon an image that makes you go 'Woohoo!', tear out the page.
● Make a pile of your finds.
● Warning: don't take an image unless it immediately makes you feel euphoric. If you hesitate, turn the page – even if it takes going through thirty magazines to find two images, this is very important.
● Once you have about two hundred images, no less, take stock. Look at all these photos, drawings and texts, and eliminate half of them.
● Cut out of the pages what appealed to you the most: a word, one side of an image, part of a drawing.
● Paste them all onto your sheet of cardboard without planning it out first.
● When everything is glued on, examine the result: what does this collage say?

What type of life do you seem to desire?

● Put this mood board up in a place where you can see it every day. Take a photo of it and make it the wallpaper on your computer and smartphone.

The images say much more about your subconscious than the words do. You might not understand exactly what these images mean, but your subconscious knows, and will lead you naturally to a life that will bring you these sorts of feelings.

Challenge
Transforming yourself into a wise elder

If you were eighty years old, what would you write to the person you are today? Write yourself a letter full of good advice that will guide you.

● Gather together some paper, an envelope, a stamp and a pen.

● Set yourself up in a comfortable place.

● Close your eyes and look ahead into the future. Imagine you're eighty years old and your life is behind you. Feel the sensations in your old body, your tiredness, your resignation.

● When you're really in the skin of your character, start to write a letter addressed to the current-day you.

● Don't think: just let your hand express itself. Don't hold back, just write what comes to you, even if it doesn't seem interesting to you or appears clichéd.

● If you don't feel sufficiently inspired, you could try responding to some very simple questions, along the lines of: 'What in life is important? What is it that has made me happy for all these years? What are my regrets? What would I do differently if I could have my time again?'

● There's no need to write a book – one side of a sheet of paper is just plenty. If the inspiration comes, go for it, but don't put pressure on yourself.

● Don't re-read it. Fold up the letter, put it in the envelope, add the stamp and address it to yourself.

● The day you receive this letter, take a decent amount of time to read it properly and to value its advice.

We all have within us a wiser side, a part that knows what's important and where we should go. Questioning it from time to time can help us to recentre ourselves around what's essential.

Game

And the

winner is ...

Who wants to be a millionaire?
- Have your notebook and a pen with you.
- Make yourself comfortable.
- Close your eyes and imagine that you've won thirty-six million in the lottery.
- That's right, thirty-six million. Be really aware of everything that passes through your body at the announcement of this news. How would your accountant respond? What does your family say?
- After having given money to your friends and family, invested in bricks and mortar, travelled the world and spent months or even years at the beach, that's it – you're bored.
- What do you do?
- Open your eyes and write without thinking.
- If it doesn't come, answer the following questions: What are your days like? What you do when you get up? Who do you have lunch with? What do you do with your afternoon? Who do you want to help? Who do you turn to? What exactly do you wish the world would give you, besides money?

Often, fear of not having enough blocks us from following our true vocation. We'd like to do heaps of things, but we forbid ourselves from doing them, because we imagine that they won't pay. The act of freeing yourself from this constraint for a few minutes often reveals deep, repressed longings. Even if they seem risky, often they're your true path to success. To know them is already to have taken a big step forward.

Challenge
Fulfil the needs of the world

How could the world be a better place?

● Take out your notebook and a pen.

● Imagine you have a magic wand and that you can change five things in the world. Only five.

● Write, without thinking too much about it, what those five things would be. Don't worry about the logistics of making these changes – you have a magic wand.

● Do you have your five changes? Now keep just three of them, the three that seem the most important to you.

● What could you do straightaway to start in the direction of one of your three changes? For example, if you chose that there would be no more rubbish and that people would respect the planet, ask yourself what steps you could take immediately to generate less rubbish yourself. If you wished for world peace, who could you yourself make peace with? And so on.

Discover the things that trouble you the most about today's world and put little actions in place to help you find out more about what motivates you and gives meaning to your everyday life. These topics and actions will start conversations: it's an opening towards infinite possibilities. Over to you!

Game
The stories of your life

The stories you liked and the ones that have had the greatest impact on you have a meaning to be deciphered. Let's do it!

● Remember what your favourite film/story/comic was when you were a child, the one that you re-read several times or watched over and over again. What was this story about? Which values did it call attention to?

● Now find a story that had an impact on your adolescence. Could you summarise it? What values did it convey? Who was the main character? What did you like most about them?

● Remember a story that really made sense in your life and triggered a reaction in you. What was this story? In what ways did it move you so much that it had an impact on your life?

And recently, which story have you liked? A novel? A play? A film? What was the topic? What about it had an impact on you?

These stories and characters that have punctuated your existence: what do they have in common? Could you find three points in common between them all?

Recognising yourself in a character or liking a story is not insignificant. Each reveals different facets of your personality and the subjects that affect you deeply.

Magic

Your successes
to come

In light of what you've discovered this week, now let's discover your objectives in life.

● Take up your notebook and a pen.

● Do a little dance of satisfaction to put you in the frame of mind of someone who's accomplished something important.

● Then, without thinking too much about it, list the ten accomplishments that you think you'll be most proud of at the end of your life. For example: producing a documentary on ecology, having two bright and happy children, painting hundreds of canvases and having them exhibited, owning a big house by the sea, and so on.

This list is your real objective in light of your progress towards your *ikigai*. In a year, you can return and modify it or add other objectives. It shows the scale and ambition of your mission. It will help you when you're looking for motivation, when you're asking yourself what it's all for.

I'M SURROUNDING MYSELF

Until now, we've consulted those around you quite rarely and we haven't made much use of your relatives either.

This week, your friends and family and also the newcomers in your life, the strangers who will cross your path, will have an important role to play in the discovery of your *ikigai*.
Their ideas, advice and opinions can finally be useful to you, now that you have a better understanding of your own and you're ready to strike a balance.

Let's think a little

t was a conversation with a stranger that made me realise a little of who I was. I was on holiday with my husband in Malibu, on the other side of the world. We had rented a little house whose pool we shared with the neighbouring house. At that time, I was in the middle of my existential search – I didn't know anymore if I should continue with photography, which earned me a living but excited me less and less; push on further as an internet influencer with a new blog; return to journalistic writing; or start again with something completely new. In short, I was lost, and very content to finally be on holidays after finishing a 5000 kilometre road trip for work, from New York to Los Angeles.

We'd hardly put our suitcases down before I hurried to the swimming pool I'd been anticipating for so long. Already lying beside the water was the couple with whom we'd be sharing our idyllic sojourn. Eager to swim, I'd rushed down, but my husband was taking his time. And so I found myself – me, the shy person – more or less obliged to establish the initial contact with our neighbours. Luckily, it was Easton who opened the conversation, and at the end of five minutes of small talk, he asked: 'When did you know that you wanted to be an artist?' Funny question. Especially coming from someone who had no clue at all about what I did – we'd only talked about our trip and where we were from. A very interesting question too. Thinking aloud, I told him about my drawing classes as a child, my choosing fine arts rather than social sciences, about wandering into fashion, from photography to styling and artistic direction, and about my attraction to writing. He talked to me about his paintings, his first exhibition, his late epiphany, how he came back to painting after numerous fruitless detours. We talked about inspiration and new ideas: this American painter who exhibits throughout the world had no doubt whatsoever that I was his equal. This conversation renewed my confidence in my creativity. Without guiding me in one direction or another, it set me back on track and made me own the fact that even if I had no one precise discipline, I was, through my state of mind, my way of seeing life and my quirky ideas, a natural artist. It was a complete stranger making me his equal that returned me to my rightful place. This conversation helped me progress much more than all the skill assessments, brainstorming with friends and other fact-finding I had done. Sometimes, talking to someone else can teach you more about yourself than the sum total of all your introspection.

Your inner circle

All around you, you have people who you know very well: your parents, certain members of your family you're particularly close to, certain old friends who've followed all your adventures for years. While their received ideas about you could have been bad for you at the outset of your quest, now, with the knowledge you've acquired about yourself, you can open yourself up to their vision of things. Since they love you and you're someone central to their lives, you can enlist them and ask for their help. From a brainstorming family meeting where each person lists your qualities and reflects on what you could do with them, to a tour of some of their professions, it's time to get them involved this week.

Newcomers

Often, when we work on our personal development – as you yourself are doing, since you have this book in your hands right now – we draw people to us, have chance meetings, discover people who are in the same state of mind as us or others who've advanced much further. This process of seeking to improve yourself, of opening yourself up to the world in a different way, allows you to change your point of view and thus to get closer to people who may already be where you are trying to go. Your search for your *ikigai* has opened up a world of new conversations and new things to have in common, which are also opportunities to get new people to become part of your circle. This new circle that you're in the process of bringing together is a little more like the real you. They're people you've chosen, people who, like you, are eager to improve themselves and advance. They can help you to renew your motivation on your days of doubt, to see more clearly into a situation than you can, to take a step back in looking at your quest. Have fun bringing them together, introducing them to each other, even organising themed evenings based on your search for your *ikigai*. Nothing beats power in numbers for untangling the challenges that life throws at you!

Strangers

Strangers are the people who cross your path but don't become part of your circle for various reasons: geographic distance, not enough in common, not enough time to really get to know each other, no availability on your part or theirs. These people will never be your close friends, but they'll nevertheless prove indispensable in your current quest. This week, strike up conversations with strangers – we'll learn how to do this in the second part of this chapter. These conversations will allow you to obtain a completely neutral point of view: a stranger doesn't care if you're doing better than they are, if you're a better or more interesting person – there's no rivalry or blocking. A stranger isn't trying to get you on their side; they have no vested interest. A stranger can have fresh ideas, come from a field you don't know at all and find a completely new meaning for your existence. None of what they say should be taken as gospel, but gathering diverse opinions is essential at this stage of your journey.

People you admire

If you have the possibility of connecting in some way with some people you admire, you can take a big leap forward in your search. As we've seen in the preceding weeks, the people we admire are often an idealised version of ourselves. Delve into this question as seriously as you can. Do you admire Zadie Smith? Try to understand why. What about her do you envy? What exactly about her actions and what you know of her speaks to you so much that you feel this attraction even though you've never met her?

Among the people you admire, and whose journey you envy, surely some are accessible to you. The most highly publicised people are hard to access, so aim primarily for people who aren't necessarily well known. If the people who impress you most are very high profile, you can perhaps reach them through social media. If you have the chance of an email exchange or, even better, to meet one of these people you admire, this will help you greatly on your quest. Someone you regard so highly will inevitably point you in a good direction.

Moai,
five allies for life

On the island of Okinawa, which brought us the concept of *ikigai*, each child is allocated a clan: five people, of mixed ages, are designated as responsible for each other. Like godfathers and godmothers, but more of them, and much longer lasting! This clan meets regularly – in childhood to play, in adulthood to help one another. The custom ensures that people meet regularly for pleasure, but also so that each one can talk about their lives and their worries, and the others can think about their problems and offer solutions. Money is raised at the beginning of these reunions, which generally take place each month, the amount depending on the income of each member, and at the end of the meeting this pot is given to the one who needs it most. These cooperative groups are very stable. Imagine how reassuring and encouraging it would be to belong to such a clan. Could you create your own? Who around you would play this game?

Let's play a little

Let's have a closer look at your circle and see how they can help you get closer to your *ikigai*. New ways of seeing things, new points of view – this week of opening up will be a challenge!

Magic
Family brainstorming

There's nothing better than your loved ones for guiding you towards your *ikigai*.

● Bring together as many of the people you're closest to as you can, on a Sunday afternoon, for example.

● Don't hesitate to mix family and old friends.

● Be really clear in your invitation: it's to help you bring meaning to your life and find a good reason for you to get up in the morning – a themed brainstorming session.

● Set some ground rules: no hasty judgements, everyone will have time to speak, they'll do their best to explain their view in the kindest way possible.

● Start with laying the foundations by telling them about the recent discoveries you've made and explaining what stage you're at now in your thinking process.

● Ask a few questions, some of which can be pretty open-ended: 'What fields do you think I'm cut out for? In which world do you see me evolving?' Others will be more precise: 'List three of my qualities. Suggest three professions I could follow.'

● Compare points of view without reaching a quick conclusion. Judge which of them holds water and which don't work as well.

● Make a note of your conclusions in your notebook.

At worst, you will have spent some time in a different way from usual and gathered lots of information. At best, here you are, furnished with lots of new points of view and fresh paths to explore.

Challenge
Dialogue with strangers

Today you're going to talk to three strangers and discover at least three aspects of your personality. If you're shy, this challenge will seem insurmountable, but it's essential for your journey. Follow this guide and you'll see that everything goes smoothly.

● Go to a place where people stroll about and have time to spare: a park, a museum, a shopping centre. You can also capitalise on a situation where people are stuck for a while: a bus stop, waiting in line at a restaurant, the supermarket queue, and so on. If you're shy, take advantage of a situation where a stranger has a slight obligation to make conversation with you: in a taxi, at the hairdresser, having a manicure, at the bookshop or the florist …

● Right at the start, ask them a question about life that's been on your mind. For example: 'How did you know what you wanted to do in life? How did you choose what to study?'

● If this seems too abrupt or you can't face it, you can make use of a compliment: 'What a pretty dress. You've got great taste? Do you have an artistic job?' And then you can add the question you really want to ask.

● You'll probably have to approach about fifteen people in order to have three interesting exchanges.

● Listen carefully to what they say and come back to them with open questions.

● Once your conversation is over, make a note in your notebook of the points that seemed interesting to you.

The more conversations you initiate, the more experiences you'll have that will be able to inspire you. Don't hesitate to repeat the experiment over several days if you enjoyed the exercise.

Game

Quest for meaning

Since some people have already accomplished their quest, why not use them as inspiration?

- Gather together a few friends who, in your view, have succeeded in putting meaning into what they do, who have found themselves. Try to choose people who haven't known what they wanted to do since childhood, but instead have changed paths and branched out: who have questioned themselves.
- You can invite people back who've already taken part in an earlier exercise if their experiences seem relevant and they're willing to help you.
- Meet for a drink so you can talk freely.
- Go around the table and get each person to introduce themselves by saying what matters most in life for them. The next time around the table, ask each to explain how they discovered the meaning they currently find in their lives. Then, ask each to describe an important revelation they've had about why they're here, and so on.
- Record in your notebook the reflections and ideas that made an impression on you during the evening. Do this gradually – it's important to have a little distance.
- What struck you most? Why, do you think?

Listening and observing other people's journeys towards their *ikigai* can furnish you with new ideas and open up other ways of envisaging life. Compare points of view as much as possible. Don't hesitate to start a conversation about *ikigai* and the meaning of life whenever you get the chance.

Challenge
Meeting
your hero

Imagine that an admirer comes to meet you in a few years to ask you how you succeeded in revealing your true self. Wouldn't you be delighted and flattered? It's high time to bring this pleasure to the person who inspires you the most.

● Choose among the people you admire, someone who's relatively accessible – that is, someone who lives in your city, or someone who has a social media presence and who is easy to contact.

● Prepare and write in your notebook three precise questions to ask.

● Your questions must be open and allow you to see more clearly into what's blocking your own progress: choosing a direction, being sure of a vocation, motivation, values ...

● You can write to your hero, but ideally you'll be able to at least talk to them on the phone if you can't meet them in the flesh. If your hero doesn't seem available and you don't receive a response, don't insist any more than is reasonable. A few attempts to make contact, but beyond that, choose someone else.

● Straight after the meeting, make notes, mixing your impressions and their answers.

● Look over these notes in the days to come and add your conclusions: What did this meeting teach you? What can you apply? What can you use for support, motivation and reassurance?

Game
The essence of others

Find out how your friends' *ikigai* can help you find your own.

- Take up your notebook and a pen.
- List the people in your circle – those you've met recently and those you've known forever – who in your view have found their *ikigai*.
- Also list those who don't seem to be conscious of it but who, for you, clearly have an *ikigai*.
- Beside each name, try to summarise in one sentence the *ikigai* of that person.
- Underline or circle those that have the most meaning for you.
- Choose the three 'vocations' that inspire you the most.
- Find a common denominator to these *ikigai*.
- If your own *ikigai* were a fusion of these three *ikigai*, how would you formulate it in a single sentence?

What we recognise in others we can find, with a little digging, in ourselves. You're only a few steps away from your *ikigai*. Well done!

Magic

Creating your moai

Does the idea of an interdependent clan appeal to you? Do you wish you were born on Okinawa with your own *moai*? Well, create one this very day!

● Choose ten people from your circle who you really feel close to.

● 'Close' doesn't mean that you've known them for twenty years, but is based rather on your intuition, so list them without thinking about it too much.

● Organise with them an evening or a meeting one afternoon around a meal or a drink.

● Explain the objective of the meeting clearly without going into too much detail.

● Suggest to each person, in your invitation, that they bring with them one or several people who might be interested.

● On the day, make a little speech introducing the meaning of the *moai* for you and why you want to pull one together.

● Suggest to each person that they think about it and if they're interested to write their name in your notebook as they go.

● Explain clearly that the expectations are sizeable – regular meetings, unstinting mutual help and support from each member for the others – and that it's better to refuse than not to meet their obligations afterwards.

● A few days after this first meeting, get in touch with those who left their names and suggest a first get-together.

Even if there are only a few people left, you've brought together a solid circle, people you can really count on. This will give you a little more freedom and support for achieving your *ikigai*.

I'M GOING INTO ACTION

Of course, it's not as if you've been sitting on your hands for the last ten weeks, but now you're really going to face reality.

We've uncovered your past, sought to understand your drives, defined your priorities, listed your desires and dreams. Now it's all about moving forward, attempting your first steps towards the path you're drawn to.

We'll go gently, of course, with the aim of sorting out what really suits you and what should stay in the realm of fantasy.

Let's think a little

t's already been four years since I discovered who I really am, since I read all those books on personal development to find new questions and new ways of looking at myself. For a while already, I'd also been reading theoretical books on life coaching, how to help others find themselves and how to run workshops on creativity. I even took courses to become a hypnotherapist and naturopath. And yet I was still vague about finding out what I wanted to do, and how I wanted to contribute to the world. I was lost.

Thanks to a friend who is a publicist, I was invited to a lecture given to the press by a very well-known life coach. I found his speech particularly powerful. He mixed American-style motivational coaching with really spiritual words about life. He said things that seemed obvious, but that I'd never formulated in that way before. And then, as often happens when I meet someone who does something that interests me, I said to myself, 'This is it, I want to do what he does.' I wanted to be a life coach and give lectures. At the end of his presentation I asked to interview him, and then after that I asked him if he could coach me. He accepted and we made a time for the following week. In the lounge of a luxury hotel in Paris, after having listened to me for a long time, he hit my concerns right on the head when he said: 'You're afraid to take action. You see yourself as a victim and you're waiting for a solution to appear all on its own, but it doesn't work that way.' I found that a bit harsh, but I asked him: 'What can I do, practically, to get away from all that?' He started to laugh and fired back: 'How quickly can you organise to coach more than thirty people from now until the end of next month?' I thought he had some nerve answering me with a question. He added: 'You could set up your first week of coaching, since that's clearly what interests you.' I explained that I couldn't, that I hadn't finished my training and that I wasn't ready. And he retorted with something that was completely spot on, a phrase that changed everything: 'We're never ready.' Then he added: 'We can train our whole lives, and it's a very good thing to do, but you already have training in hypnotherapy and naturopathy, and real people skills. You've already mastered more things than lots of people who are practising life coaches, so I'll giving you ten minutes to think of a theme for a seminar.' The seminar never took place, but I realised that I actually did have lots of skills already and that it was time to put them into practice. To face up to reality. It was a giant leap, because it's in getting started that we learn the most. The next week I saw my first clients, and positive comments were posted on the website where people booked their coaching sessions. He was right. And how about you? What if you're more ready than you think?

The limits to searching for yourself

Looking for your true self and asking yourself good questions is an exciting quest. When, as a result, we start to see such clear improvements in our daily life, we quickly develop a taste for learning what we truly want, and discovering our strengths and weaknesses. We begin to allow ourselves to accept ourselves even when we're completely aware of who we are. Knowing that we have one or another value, one or another weakness, one or another priority, allows us to develop a certain kindness towards ourselves. The concern, however, is that this search will last our whole life long and we'll never write 'the end'. And so we have to know how to put a time limit on the process and set it aside, at least the intellectual part of it – the reading, quizzes and tests – and live. We can't spend years only thinking about things – not just for financial reasons but also for our own morale: how boring! How do you know when you've advanced far enough? It isn't obvious, which is why I gave the program in this book a precise duration. Not everyone will be at the same stage when they close this book, but each individual will have had a long enough interlude to see themselves more clearly. Nothing is stopping you from continuing, but beware of that infinite quest that absorbs you completely, and know when to say 'stop'. A good point of reference is your own fatigue: do you feel like you've reached a plateau? That you're stagnating a little? If that's the case, even if you're still not quite there with your *ikigai*, it's time to take action.

The need to face up to reality

Stopping the quest doesn't mean not making any more progress towards self-realisation. On the contrary: it's not that you won't learn any more about yourself, but just that you're changing mode, moving from questioning to action. If you stay stuck in your head, you can imagine heaps of things and make plans that aren't necessarily right. For example, you loved horseriding as a child and you want to explore it as a possible future; in fact, you can already see yourself setting up your own riding school. You should, however, be aware that you could get on a horse again and hate it. If this happens, everything will be called into question, so it's better to do it as soon as possible. Only through taking action will we understand if our projections and fantasies are realistic.

We might dream of being a florist, but after working for a week in a florist's boutique, it's possible we'll realise that the hours don't suit us, that it's less artistic than we imagined, or that dealing with clients isn't as nice as we hoped. And we could never have known that by staying at home and thinking. On the other hand, we could spend a day working in a second-hand shop and realise that we're passionate about sales, that the challenge of having someone leave with more things than they intended to buy stimulates us, and gives us immense joy. And we couldn't have worked that out without trying it. This is why, this week, it's about doing and not about thinking anymore. Even doing the things that don't really tempt you that much at first glance. Just to see. Do as much as possible. Stay open to every possibility, as if you had no idea about what really interests you. You'll always learn something.

Daring to say yes and initiating suggestions

Now is the moment to be tough with yourself. You'll have to say 'yes' to as many experiences as possible and try a maximum of things without thinking about it too much beforehand. If a friend wants you to go up with them in a hot air balloon, go for it; if your mother-in-law wants to take you mushroom hunting, dive in. This week, you're not allowed to refuse anything that comes up. Even worse, you have to ask to do more. Dare to say to those around you who do jobs you're drawn to, for whatever reason, that you'd love to know more and even to try out their daily life. Dare to try experiences that seem improbable or offbeat, because you'll always learn something about yourself, your wishes and your needs. The more you say, 'Oh no, that's too crazy, too out there, that's got nothing to do with anything', the more reason to try the thing you're talking about.

The more you open yourself up to the world, the more precise your idea will be of what you're capable of and what you really want to do with your life. In a dream we can do anything. In real life we sometimes realise that the activity we fantasised about is nothing like we imagined. It could be even more interesting, and that will give us more motivation to get some training, and will open up new possibilities. Or, on the contrary, it could turn out to be much less exciting than we anticipated, and that will mean less time wasted!

Impostor syndrome

Seventy per cent of adults have doubts at some point in their career about the legitimacy of their success, explains the psychologist Pauline Rose Clance in her book *The Impostor Phenomemon: Overcoming the Fear that Haunts Your Success* (Peachtree Publishers, 1985). Anxiety about not being good enough is therefore universal. There you go: you're less alone. If you already have an idea, even a small one, of what you could do, whether or not you really feel ready, it's high time to take the plunge. Forget your anxiety about its legitimacy – just jump in. Test the things you're drawn to in order to avoid throwing yourself into things that don't suit you at all. If you want to become a software developer, then spend some time helping a developer, if only for a day – make them coffee, answer their phone, tidy up – and discover the reality of their day-to-day life. If no one around you does this job, use social media to find someone you could observe. These days it's very easy; make the most of the advantages of this era where people are easily accessible. Are you hesitant about contacting a stranger to try out their job? Imagine the reverse situation: if someone wrote to you because they were interested in what you do and would like a bit of help, what would you do? Wouldn't you be flattered? Well then, go for it.

To find inspiration for which fields to try out, don't hesitate to make a really exhaustive list of what you like and then find an experience for each item. For example, if you love cheese: test as many cheese-linked activities as you can, from raising the animals to making and selling the cheese. You're a tennis fan? Become informed about all the jobs that have something to do with that sport, whether intimately or more distantly connected. You're passionate about psychology, but the profession of psychologist doesn't speak to you? Test everything that you could do around it – lectures, books – finding out about these things and meeting people in this field. You don't have any training? No big deal: there's always a way of trying a job, by assisting someone who does it, by simply observing them, by offering your services to your friends. There are thousands of solutions: the only real obstacle is your fear, so forget about it. Come to terms with putting it aside and try what tempts you most. At best, your excitement about the field will be encouraged and you can then do everything possible to keep moving in that direction; at worst, you won't like it and you'll avoid wasting your time and money doing the training.

Kaizen, the theory of little steps

The Japanese word *kaizen* breaks down into two parts: *kai*, which means 'change', and *zen*, which means 'better'. It describes a process of continual improvement, a method used a lot in Japanese businesses, but also increasingly in the West. This way of doing things can be completely transferred from the work context and applied to your personal life. It's about taking little steps towards getting better without turning everything upside down or calling your habits into question too much. It's therefore much easier to maintain in the long term. For example, for someone who'd like to start exercising, the first step would be taking the stairs rather than the elevator. Then, when this habit has been acquired, doing a ten-minute brisk walk one morning a week, then fifteen minutes, then twice a week, then for thirty minutes. The progression seems logical and good habits are put in place gradually. If we started straight off with the objective of doing a thirty-minute brisk walk twice a week, it's very unlikely we'd manage it, especially in the long term.

Let's play a little

To take action, nothing beats a few exercises. This week particularly, make a real effort with the games and go as far as possible. It won't be easy, but you'll learn a lot about yourself and your true desires. There's nothing better for putting a stop to doubt than trying things out, so go for it!

Game

Bucket list

What would you like to do before you die? Why not start doing it today?
- Take your notebook and a pen.
- Make a list of everything you'd like to have done by the time you die.
- Prioritise the items with three levels of urgency: 1. as soon as possible, 2. a bit later, 3. it can wait for a little bit longer.

- Take your list of urgent 1s and make a date in less than three months to have done each one of the things on your list. For example: do a parachute jump next Sunday; visit another city on the last weekend of the month, and so on.
- Try to program at least one activity this week, the earlier the better.
- For what's not feasible in the next three months for reasons of budget and/or organisation, find a way to make the plan a reality nevertheless. For example, if you want to see the Great Wall of China, find out the price of a trip to China; look at when you could go, what your budget would be and how you could get the money together; research hotels or alternative accommodation; and ideally fix a date and find a quote for an airline ticket. In short, make this trip much more real.

Making our desires and dreams a reality is very stimulating. It's an excellent way to develop even more ideas and to realise how accessible they actually are.

Magic
Action!

Do you moan a lot? Today is going to be very useful to you!

• From the morning onwards, spot whenever you start to moan or complain about something.

• Have your notebook with you throughout the day to take notes.

• At the moment you start complaining, note the subject of your complaint and its level of seriousness.

• Don't do anything else.

• When the evening comes, look back over your notes: Does the same reason for complaining come up regularly? What are your most unpleasant complaints?

• Beside each complaint, write three actions you could put in place to make them disappear. For example: you complain that all your clothes tumble out whenever you open your wardrobe. Perhaps you could have a clean-out, arrange things better or invest in more storage. If you complain about being cold, maybe you could do more exercise to warm up your body, or be better informed about the weather so you can dress more suitably and invest in a few really warm items of clothing.

• As quickly as possible, put these solutions into action.

We complicate life to avoid taking action and we put up with daily inconveniences so as not to call anything into question. But doesn't it feel better to finally take things into your own hands? What if you applied this approach to your whole life in a bigger sense?

Challenge

*Action at
every stage*

Now you have been enriched by your experience of the beneficial effects of action, today let's attack something bigger: the construction site of your life.

- Take your notebook and a pen, and note everything you'd like to improve in your life in a very general way: from your love relationship to the substance of your job and your family relationships, to your mood or your ability to bounce back.

- Make a really long list of all the things you'd like to be better. As always, don't censor yourself, even if an item seems absurd or ridiculous.

- Number each of the items on your list to give them an order of priority.

- For the first three, as for the last exercise, find, without thinking about it too much, three ideas to make progress with the situation. For example: if you'd like to have better communication with your partner, perhaps you could take a course in non-violent communication, see a therapist as a couple or on your own, or even read books and watch lectures on communication within relationships.

- Out of all your actions, carry one out today – for example, read a book about communication – and make dates for the others so you can do some planning on how to make them happen in advance. For example: look up the dates for the next courses in non-violent communication and find out how to sign up so that you can decide on an opportune moment to start taking action.

When we do start to take action, it's so stimulating that it becomes easier and easier. The act of facing up to the subjects that preoccupy you and succeeding at making progress with them is a fantastic source of motivation. I'll bet you that all at once you'll sort out a heap of things that have been dragging on for a really long time. Goodbye, procrastination!

Game
Don't be afraid

Say goodbye to fear and hello to challenges!

● Choose someone you trust to play with you, ideally someone who also needs to take more action and have less fear in their life.

● List the ten little things that scare you and are blocking you at the moment. For example: 'I can't bear to tell my mother that I don't want to go to her place for Christmas this year', or 'I'd like to drastically reduce the quantity of meat in my diet but I'm afraid of my husband's reaction', or even 'I'd like to learn salsa dancing but I'm too scared of looking ridiculous, starting at my age'.

● The more specific you are, the more beneficial this exercise will be. Clearly define the causes and the possible consequences. In other words, say something like: 'I never got my driver's licence because I'm too afraid of failing, of wasting all that money and disappointing my family,' rather than 'I'm afraid of doing my driving test' or 'I'm afraid of failing my driving test.'

● From this list, your partner in the game will choose the fear that you're going to confront this week. Conversely, you'll choose the fear that they must overcome.

● Support each other, and give each other advice and ideas to tackle the different fears. When we're on the outside, we often have excellent ideas.

● Tell each other about your adventures, how you've overcome your fear or not, what happened, how you dealt with it, and the reactions you had.

Having the support of someone who's in a similar situation to yours is a real motivator. If your duo functions well, go on to the next item on your list, doing, say, about one a month, and discover how powerful you can be when you take action!

Nothing is better than a real pro to get you on the right track.

- Choose a job you dream about having. Even if it's not in a profession you've particularly considered pursuing, but something that you fantasise about and would love to know more about.

- Think about your friends. Is there someone who does this job or could be close to it? For example, if the dream job is midwife, and you have a pregnant friend, that's already one way in.

- When you find someone who does the job, ask them if you can spend a day observing them. Of course, if possible you can act as their assistant for the day.

- Don't be offended if they say no. In certain fields, it can be very tricky or complex to welcome a person from the outside. If this happens, try asking other professionals.

- If there's really no professional who wants you to spend the day with them, ask them for an interview, even over the phone, and ask them as many practical and realistic questions as you can about their daily life.

- You can also look for a realistic documentary, so ask the professionals who can't take you on to give you advice on something to watch or read.

- Gather as much information as possible. What's their daily work routine like? The atmosphere? What are the hours? The obligations? The advantages?

- Then take stock. What was it that attracted you so much? Is the attraction still as strong after this day or this new information? Even more so? A little less? Why?

Seeing more clearly into a 'dream' job can allow us to put things into perspective and confront our fantasy with real-life proof. If you don't like working at night, it will be difficult for you to do certain jobs, even if you can imagine moving mountains to get there. If you're well aware of all the downsides of a job and you still feel drawn to it, it's a real pathway to explore.

Challenge
The stop button

Are you getting a bit tired now of taking action with everything? That's good: today, inertia is your friend.

● You'll need an hour free to do this challenge seriously. Don't allow anyone to disturb you, and turn off your phone and the internet.

● Press the 'stop' button: stop your thoughts, stop your fears, stop being active no matter what.

● For an hour, your aim is to do nothing. At all.

● Don't look at a screen, or your phone, or whatever piece of technology it might be.

● You are not allowed to do any cleaning, or the dishes or tidying up or organising.

● You must not buy anything, do any window-shopping or go out anywhere.

● You're also not allowed to do an abs session or ride your exercise bike, or any other exercise.

● For the first half-hour, you can perhaps meditate, do some breathing exercises, be conscious of the passage of time, work on being in the present.

● Don't do too much; it's mainly about taming your boredom.

● For the second half-hour, you can write your impressions in your notebook, recording everything that goes through your head.

Pushing procrastination and inactivity to the extreme allows us to realise how essential it is to be active. It's also a way of reminding yourself that it's good to take a break from time to time, because that's when we have the best ideas.

Magic
Go with the flow

It's really good to work towards a goal. But often, when we're working on our personal development, we feel a bit lost and don't always know which direction to take. This exercise will help you move forward and take action even if you don't have a particular objective.

● This morning, or this afternoon if that's more convenient for you, you're going to rely on nothing but flow for three hours.

● Flow is when your desires meet reality. For example, if you suddenly feel like eating an avocado sandwich, just like that, even though it's not lunchtime, listen to your desire and make yourself that sandwich.

● Pay attention, a little like during one of the very first exercises in the first chapter, when it was about listening to the desires your body suggested and to all the signals from your five senses.

● For three hours, you must do everything to put your desires into action.

● If you want to go and browse books at a bookstore, do it. If you feel like going for a jog, go on. And if, in the middle of jogging, you dream about drinking a smoothie, stop running. Follow the flow without resisting it at all.

● Don't force yourself into anything, don't accept an invitation that doesn't tempt you, don't go against your will.

● If you don't feel anything and you have no particular desire, you can go for a random stroll – toss a coin to go left or right, and see where it leads you.

● At the end of your three hours of great freedom, record in your notebook what happened, what you're proud of, what you were doubtful about, and ask yourself: were there any miracles? (You found a banknote that allowed you to buy a new item of clothing? You bumped into someone you've been wanting to see but hadn't plucked up the courage to call? You discovered a lovely little park near your house? And so on.)

Going with the flow isn't always possible in daily life. We must, however, try to do it as much as possible, because it opens up opportunities for beautiful surprises and the chance to discover new interests.

Books for taking the plunge

For allowing yourself to do more things:
21 Rituals to Change Your Life, Theresa Cheung,
Watkins Publishing, 2017

For understanding the degree to which we have
an impact on our life:
*Declutter Your Mind: How to Stop Worrying, Relieve
Anxiety, and Eliminate Negative Thinking*, S.J. Scott &
Barrie Davenport, 2016

For changing our outlook on life:
*We Can Be Kind: Healing Our World One Kindness at a
Time*, David Friedman, AP Editions, 2017
*Happiness Is A Choice You Make: Lessons From a Year
Amongst Our Oldest Old*, John Leland, Sarah Crichton
Books, 2018

I'M
RADIANT

Here you are, ready for the revelation – which can now really only be one thing – after having cleared the way for it, bit by bit.

You will already have started to have an idea of what your *ikigai* could be.

This week, we're going to see how, enriched by all this new knowledge about yourself, you can have a better idea of why you get up each morning, and finally be able to shine.

Let's think a little

My *ikigai* has evolved a lot since I first found it. You mustn't be afraid to jump in and formulate a statement that will have to change later – the key is to begin. Mine clicked for me after a long period of introspection, but also after a break where I couldn't read any more books on personal development. It was when I was watching a lecture on the meaning of life that I said to myself: 'That's it, it's high time I managed to put into words what gives life meaning for me.' I took a notebook and a pencil, and I wrote lots of sentences going in every direction, full of ideas that at first glance were incoherent. I read over my old notes from when I was searching for my values, my ideas for the future and my desire for change in the world and, with some digging, I found it. I found an *ikigai* sentence. It was long and a little convoluted, which made it far from perfect, but I had something. I set it aside for a few days then came back to it and radically changed the formulation, simplifying it and making it lighter. I still wasn't completely satisfied with it, though. It was only a few months later that I finally found the one that still works for me today: 'My *ikigai* is to steer the world towards more beauty, joy and gentleness through my creativity.'

I never could have imagined how much this simple little statement was going to change my life. On a personal front, I finally have an opinion on things, having never dared before to offer one, as I thought that other people's opinions were more important. These days, I know that I'd like to soften the world and make it lighter, and so I'm doing it, I'm going for it. I dare to respond, to say what I see in a situation, to make my contribution to the conversation. On a professional front, I also know now exactly what I'm looking for. As a result, when what I'm doing isn't pointing me in the right direction, I change it.

I see my entire journey more clearly, and I've realised that in reality, without knowing it, I'd often put my *ikigai* to work already. When I was a radio announcer with FIP, I brought gentleness with my voice and joy with my light-hearted shows. When I was a journalist in women's media, I brought joy to those who read my work. When I was a fashion blogger, I often mocked the fashion scene's standards to make my readers laugh. When I was a photographer, I tried to make people smile with my photos and my aesthetic was very gentle. As a life coach, I try to make my clients happy, to make their lives sweeter.

In short, without being aware of it, I was already going in more or less the right direction. Realising that fact gave me enormous confidence in life and reinforced my conviction that I'm here for a reason. It's no longer about being shy or not, intelligent or not, eloquent or not; its just about applying what I think is my mission and acting in a way that's consistent with my values. This gives me incredible strength. Now it's your turn!

The fear of shining and the damage modesty does

In many Western cultures, it's considered good to keep a low profile, whatever the situation might be. If we shine brightly, it's best not to show it. Do you earn lots of money? It's probably wise not to say so. Have you ever asked yourself why we hide our light like this? What are we afraid of? Jealousy? Envious people? Even so, does that mean we should deny our reality? Let's take a tree as an example. A tree doesn't say to itself: 'Oh, I have to make sure I don't grow too tall so I don't annoy my neighbour.' It grows, spreads out, fills out and plays its role as a tree. It's the same for you. Not only do you have the right to be good at something you like, and to do something you like doing, but you actually have a duty to do so. Applying your *ikigai* allows you to overcome this false modesty, which has no advantages for us. I'm not saying that you should become full of yourself, just that it's vital to give yourself permission to shine. By trying to extinguish your talents, by responding: 'It's nothing, it's easy, it's not really anything to do with me', you stop other people benefiting from what you can bring them. Opt for generosity, for giving of yourself; stop blocking yourself with excuses; offer your talents to the world and open the curtains wide.

The world needs your unique skills

The extraordinary thing about your *ikigai* is that it's almost always unique. It brings together skills and desires that are yours alone, and these are exactly what the world needs. There's no 'Who am I to deserve success?', but rather 'Who am I to refuse to offer my gifts to the world?' Have a look around you: how many people have exactly the same strengths, the same values and the same desires as you? Very few. In fact, none. This is why it's essential to really know yourself. In that way you can come to terms with throwing yourself into something that might otherwise seem impossible. Forget statistics and idioms: 'Yes, but you know, only two hundred people in the country make a living from that profession', or 'Many are called, but few are chosen.' Set your doubts aside and finally give to the world what you're here for.

The joy of feeling involved

Is there any greater joy than really believing that you're contributing to the world? Think over those moments in your life when you experienced this feeling of wellbeing and accomplishment. Perhaps it occurred within your family when you helped someone, or maybe through creating something. Whatever the context and the means, what matters is feeling useful. It's one of the most important needs in Maslow's hierarchy of needs, which classifies the essential human requirements. The need for esteem, which includes feeling useful to society, comes just after the physiological needs for safety and belonging: eating, sleeping, having a roof over your head, having a family, being part of a group.

Can you measure the importance of respecting your *ikigai* and making the best contribution you can according to your talents and desires?

Teru teru bozu, the doll that makes the sun shine

On rainy days, the Japanese have a custom of hanging a little paper doll in their window to make the sun come back. *Teru* means 'shine' and *bōzu* 'a Buddhist monk'. As they hang their doll, they say a little prayer asking it to make the rain go away and threatening it, in the last stanza, with cutting off its head if it doesn't succeed. The legend comes from a Buddhist monk who promised, after a long period of rain, the return of the sun in response to his prayers. When he failed, he was beheaded.

Here's the complete prayer:
Teru teru bōzu, teru bōzu
Make tomorrow a sunny day
Like the sky in a dream sometime
If it's fine, I'll give you a golden bell

Teru teru bōzu, teru bōzu
Make tomorrow a sunny day
If you make my wish come true
We'll drink lots of sweet sake (amazake)

Teru teru bōzu, teru bōzu
Make tomorrow a sunny day
Because if it's cloudy and you make it rain
I'll have to cut off your head

On the days when you refuse to shine, hang a little doll in your window to remind yourself that only you have the power to give to the world the gifts you possess. To bring the sun back into your life and the lives of other people, embody the *teru teru bōzu* for your circle.

Let's play a little

T his week, we're finally going to finish the long search to find your *ikigai*. No pressure: you can do these exercises again later; you can change them or find others. It's simply a matter of starting to give some substantial form to everything you've come to understand over the past weeks.

Magic

Write your ikigai sentence

Let's return to some of the paths we took over the preceding weeks and finally formulate your *ikigai*.

• Take your notebook and prepare yourself for diving back into your various notes.

• At your own pace, go back over the conclusions from the exercises in the previous chapters to answer the questions below. You can also answer spontaneously if that comes naturally to you.

• You can re-use the answers you've already found or update them. You can also take no notice of your old answers – feel completely free either way.

• Don't put too much pressure on yourself; you can rewrite your *ikigai* as many times as you need to. It's simply a matter of getting down a rough idea.

• The four questions you must answer are:

1. If you were only allowed to do three activities, what would they be?

2. Which of your qualities are you proudest of?

3. Which values are so important in your eyes that you'd be ready to do anything to defend them?

4. In your view, what does the world need in order to make it a better place?

• Now write your sentence: My *ikigai* is to [answer 1], thanks to [answer 2] for a world [answers 3 and 4].

● Simplify it as much as possible, leaving behind only what seems true to you today. Change the order and modify it as much as you like.

● Bear in mind the idea that it must both accurately represent the essence of what truly matters to you and be able to be understood by a six-year-old child.

Even if you're still not completely satisfied with your formulation, adopt this *ikigai*, if only temporarily. You can modify it gradually during the week, depending on your experience and your feelings, then come back to it from time to time after that as your vision evolves.

Challenge
An ikigai day

Today is about living according to your *ikigai* and putting it to the test in real life.

● As much as possible, talk about your *ikigai* with strangers, your loved ones, your colleagues and your friends.

● Ask them their opinion; whether they recognise you in that sentence; and what parts of it seems to them the most apt and the least true.

● Try as much as possible to apply your *ikigai* throughout your day. For example, if your *ikigai* is: 'I sing and I dance thanks to my sensitivity, my creativity and my aesthetic need to make the world more beautiful and sensitive', sing and dance as often as possible during your day, but also see how you sing and dance through your other activities. Do you bring creativity and beauty to organising and tidying your apartment? Do you give a sense of beauty to your students in teaching them history? Do you allow other people to express their sensitivity or their sense of beauty through what you say to them?

● Spot all the moments when you can put your *ikigai* to work, even with things that seem to be insignificant.

● Also spot the moments when you find no place at all for your *ikigai*. You can then try to work out how to apply it, and in what ways it might be possible to modify the situation a little bit.

● How could you incorporate even more of your *ikigai* into your life?

Through your actions? Through an attitude?

Whether you apply your *ikigai* close to 100 per cent of the time or you've realised how complex it is to integrate it into your life every day, you've come a long way along the path to self-realisation. Now it's only a question of slight adjustments.

Game

Ikigai
Flashback

Do you regret not having found your *ikigai* earlier? How about we go back in time a little?

• Take your notebook and make a little list of the different jobs you've done and the various milestones you've lived through (the birth of your children, getting married, moving house, and so on).

• For each of these events, try to find three points that show that you were already applying your *ikigai*. For example, if your *ikigai* consists of tidying, organising and classifying things thanks to an innate sense of order and a need for balance and calm, to make the world simpler and more settled, did you perhaps apply it already when you were studying for your degree and you organised your revision? Or in your first paying job as an assistant?

• If it doesn't seem obvious to you straightaway, see if there's an aspect of your *ikigai* that you used at the time.

Verifying that your *ikigai* was already with you, even if you hadn't yet identified it, is very reassuring: although you don't yet have the exact formulation, its essence is within you.

Challenge

*Initiate the
conversation*

Enriched by your *ikigai*, go to a networking evening* or similar and make note of how much people listen to you.

● Choose one of those networking evenings where you didn't know how to introduce yourself before.

● Speak to as many people as possible.

● To introduce yourself and explain what you do, say your *ikigai* sentence.

● Observe the reactions, and see what sorts of questions people ask you.

● The more you approach new people, the more interesting feedback you'll get on your sentence.

● When you get home, note what bothered you, what pleased you and how you felt.

Did you spot something in your sentence that needs to be adjusted, in light of the reactions you got? Take your time, and over the days that follow, make a note of how you could enrich or modify your sentence to make it more appropriate.

Game

*Essential
questions*

Already, in week 10, we took inspiration from the *ikigai* of the people around you. This time, we're going to look for inspiration in a broader way.

● Take yourself out to a networking event or an evening gathering where there will be lots of new people you don't know.

● Take your notebook with you.

* Networking evenings are gatherings where people meet around a theme, for example: 'new types of management', where you might find human resource executives, businesspeople, managers and so on. The evenings can be organised around a single profession, for example: at 'a naturopaths' evening', all naturopaths, naturopathy students and anyone interested in the subject can come to meet each other. Facebook lists lots of events of this sort, as do networking websites such as meetup.com and eventbrite.com – just enter the professions or themes that interest you in the search box.

- Before getting there, write three questions you're going to ask as many people as you can. These questions must touch on what's most important for the people you're speaking to.
- For example: what things revolt you most in the world? In your view, what change does the world need most? If you were rich, what would you do with your life?
- You can absolutely play this game the same evening you do the 'Initiate the conversation' challenge.
- Every now and again, take a moment to note what calls out to you in the answers people give you.
- When you get home, take stock: are there ideas you'd like to rework? Are there new things you'd like to incorporate into your *ikigai*? List whatever seems interesting to add.

A general survey of other people's ambitions, ideas and desires helps you to find your place and find inspiration. Did this confirm your *ikigai* or do you instead have the impression that you forgot lots of things? Sleep on it, then reformulate it!

Magic
The magic formula

Having put your *ikigai* to the reality test, it's time, with the new information you've obtained, to rewrite it.

- Lying down comfortably, re-read your whole notebook.
- Gradually list the things from your reading that seem like the most important pieces of information to keep.
- Go over your feelings this week: what's missing from your sentence that stops you from adopting it completely?
- Formulate ten sentences that could be your *ikigai*.
- Read these ten sentences aloud. Which one of them sounds the most suitable?
- Choose one, in the knowledge that this time you're going to keep it for three months. You can return to it after that time but not before. Here you are with your reworked *ikigai* formula. You should be proud!

Game

Mirror

In order to assert your *ikigai* in the world, it's good to believe it yourself.

● Stand in front of a mirror.

● Take your notebook and write three statements authorising you to live your *ikigai* fully.

● For example, if your *ikigai* is 'To write and to simplify new discoveries thanks to my talent for synthesising information and my writing abilities, in order to make the world better informed and aware', you can write: 'I have the right to live from my writing', 'I have the right and the duty to inform the world of what I've discovered', 'I have the right to earn my living by providing the world with a great service.'

● Once you have your three phrases, stand up straight and proclaim them aloud with conviction while looking into your eyes in the mirror.

● If you don't feel a great enough conviction, start again, or rewrite your statements and then start again.

As soon as you have the slightest doubt about your legitimacy, repeat this exercise. Not only do you have the right to achieve self-realisation through your *ikigai*, but most importantly, you have a duty to do so. This is your role in the world.

Conclusion

Thank you for attentively following this program, which I created in order to share with you my experience and my journey towards greater wellbeing. If you're reading this page, you've probably reached the end of your twelve weeks of reflection. Well done! I hope they were as informative as you had hoped when you opened this book. You've followed the whole program, so you definitely know much more about yourself than you did a few months ago, and most importantly you've found your *ikigai*.

Perhaps it's imperfect; perhaps you're still not completely convinced, but you have a foundation. With your *ikigai*, you're now one of those people lucky enough to have a good reason for getting up in the morning. This reason belongs to you, and it will evolve with you: it's a reflection of your desires and values.

Bravo. You knew how to put an end to a life that wasn't satisfying enough in your eyes, and you decided to search for the best way of progressing in your own way, at your own pace, in your own direction. Knowing what you really want, understanding what's essential for you, and not for your loved ones or your neighbours, is a really beautiful first step towards a life that's more genuine, more active and more surprising. Less procrastination, more true desires, fewer doubts, greater lightness. It's no longer about surviving, obeying, playing the victim of a life you don't want; it's time to take back the reins and make some important decisions.

In the months to come, your life will change, or at least your point of view regarding your life will evolve and adjust to suit your *ikigai*. With this compass in your pocket, allow yourself to be guided. Your *ikigai* is your direction: put trust in life for the rest. If, along the way, you encounter difficulties, doubts, complex choices or dilemmas, your *ikigai* will help you see more clearly. Observe, think, feel what will take you towards your *ikigai*. You just have to follow your instinct, then let yourself be surprised.

So here you are, ready to live fully, without a safety net, and to sow the seeds of true feeling; to become an inspiration for change, a creator of contagious joy. Go for it – the world is waiting for you!

About the author

Caroline de Surany is an author, life coach and speaker. Optimistic, curious and creative, she has worked in numerous professions: as a radio host, blogger (Caroline Daily), journalist for women's publications (writing on beauty, wellbeing and psychology), author of guidebooks and comics, scriptwriter and motivational speaker. She decided, during a trip to India, to change her life and become a certified life coach, reiki master, naturopath, hypnotherapist and aromatherapist. She is a minimalist convert but not to the extreme; on the way to zero waste (although still far from her goal); and a great follower of wabi-sabi, the art of appreciating the beauty of time passing.